SUPER DOG TRICKS

Inspiring | Educating | Creating | Entertaining

Brimming with creative inspiration, how-to projects, and useful information to enrich your everyday life, Quarto Knows is a favorite destination for those pursuing their interests and passions. Visit our site and dig deeper with our books into your area of interest: Quarto Creates, Quarto Cooks, Quarto Homes, Quarto Lives, Quarto Drives, Quarto Explores, Quarto Gifts, or Quarto Kids.

First Published in 2021 by Quarry Books,
an imprint of The Quarto Group,
100 Cummings Center, Suite 265-D,
Beverly, MA 01915, USA.
T (978) 282-9590 F (978) 283-2742 QuartoKnows.com

Quarry Books titles are also available at discount for retail, wholesale, promotional, and bulk purchase. For details, contact the Special Sales Manager by email at specialsales@quarto.com or by mail at The Quarto Group, Attn: Special Sales Manager, 100 Cummings Center, Suite 265-D, Beverly, MA 01915, USA.

10 9 8 7 6 5 4 3 2 1

ISBN: 978-0-76037-190-9

Digital edition published in 2021
eISBN: 978-0-76037-191-6

Library of Congress Cataloging-in-Publication Data available

Design and Page Layout: Amy Sly

Photography: Pratt + Kreidich Photography

Printed in China

SUPER DOG TRICKS

Make Your Dog a Super Dog with Step-by-Step Tricks and Training Tips

Sara Carson
Featuring the Super Collies

QUARRY

CONTENTS

INTRODUCTION

While this book is about dog tricks, it's actually written for anyone who wants to build a better relationship with a dog. Through training, a dog learns to look to his handler for guidance, which helps with his or her everyday life. It also creates a strong bond between the dog and the human, as each learns to trust the other in new ways.

Trick training has not only bettered the lives of my dogs, but it has also improved my own mental health. Learning to communicate effectively with a dog teaches patience, timing, and compassion, and encourages cooperation between two different species.

When I was a young girl, trick training was something I discovered by accident—I was quickly hooked. I worked hard to come up with creative ways to train fun and unique tricks. Spending time with my cocker spaniel and teaching him various activities was something we both enjoyed. I found online videos and books, which helped teach me how to train new tricks, but I was also sure that there were other, easier ways to achieve the same results.

Taking what I learned from both online and reading, I opened up my own dog-training business at the age of fifteen to gain more hands-on experience. In the five years that I ran Paws Up Dog Training, I worked with well over two thousand clients and their dogs. During this time, I also attended college full-time to earn a degree in graphic design, which proved extremely useful, as it allowed me to tackle all the advertising and design work necessary to be successful. I didn't always believe that I could create a career out of my passion for training dogs, so I considered my degree in graphic design my "backup."

Turns out, all the videos I made to help market myself also created an incredible opportunity for me—I was offered a full-time position traveling and performing with my dog. Finally, I knew that my dream, which had been called "silly" and "unrealistic" for so long, had actually become a reality. Anytime I hit that stage, big or small, I embraced it as a reminder—not only to myself, but also to anyone out there with a passion of their own—to never give up on your dreams.

When I wanted to move from Canada to the United States, I was told it would be next to impossible, and I simply met the challenge head-on. I had my dog Hero by my side, and I was more than ready to start a new adventure with him. We had several amazing opportunities come our way, such as appearing on *Late Show with David Letterman*, competing in *America's Got Talent*, and being a part of several national commercials. As we continued on our journey together, we learned and grew as a team. Over time, our family gradually increased in size and our life continued to change constantly. I am so incredibly thankful for this amazing dog and for the patience and companionship he has shown me through some of the hardest years of my life.

In this book, I'm sharing all of my favorite tricks, along with some of my best tips and ideas to help make training fun for both ends of the leash. Even if you want to skip most of the fundamentals in Chapter 1, take a quick look at page 10 for key terms and concepts used in this book. Then go ahead and browse the tricks in Chapters 2–4. If a trick requires your dog to already know a skill, such as sit, it will be clearly noted.

Once your dog has mastered a few tricks, check out Chapter 5, which shares a home-friendly version of freestyle! This is something you may have seen on TV (think a dog and handler going through a choreographed routine). All you need are a few tricks and music (okay, and maybe costumes!) to put on your own show.

FIND ME ONLINE

Keep track of your dog's progress by using Puppr, my free-to-download app on IOS & Android! Visit www.Puppr.app.

The app includes all sorts of things that work well with this book, including:

- Real-time chat with me for subscribers to get training questions answered

- Puppr Shop, which includes hand-picked product recommendations to help with training

- Ability to set recurring reminders for things such as a potty schedule or training sessions

- Photo challenges

- Badges to earn as you progress in your training

You can also find me on various social media sites under @TheSuperCollies and @TheSuperColliesMom and on my own website: www.thesupercollies.com. I hope you enjoy this book, whether you and your dog are attempting your very first trick or are working your way up to those impressive and acrobatic tricks—or even a whole routine.

Happy training!
Sara Carson

SUPER STARTS

What you teach your dog first is important. Whether you have a puppy or an older dog in a new situation, he is likely to be at his most impressionable. Working on the basics is crucial, and helping your dog solidify behaviors that are useful day in and out will create a solid foundation for everything else you teach him. It will help your dog have a clear understanding of what's expected of him. And a dog that understands what his family wants and expects from him, while still being allowed to make good choices, will be able to live a relaxed and happy life with his humans!

TRAINING WORDS USED IN THIS BOOK

While this chapter will teach you all sorts of basics, I realize there will be some dog owners who want to skip straight to the tricks. With that in mind, these first two sections, Key Words and Food Drive, are the only essential reading before you tackle whatever catches your eye from the trick chapters.

Throughout the tricks, you'll encounter these Key Words, which have specific meanings, the details of which can vary trainer to trainer. I always use food when training; for example, when I lure or jackpot, I am using dry kibble (for more on food and food drive, read the next section as well!):

- **LURE:** Guiding a dog, using food, to entice him to follow the reward

- **MARK:** A sound/word (for example, "yes") that is used to indicate that the dog has done a behavior that will earn a reward (again, I recommend using food)

- **JACKPOT:** A large reward of food (or multiple small pieces of food, one immediately after another) to indicate a behavior has been done very well

- **GESTURE:** Using a part of your body (for example, your hand) to help guide your dog

- **CUE:** A signal to the dog to perform a specific behavior. Note that there are several types of cues. Verbal and hand signals are two examples you'll find throughout this book.

- **RELEASE CUE:** The signal to a dog that the behavior he is currently doing (e.g., stay) is completed and he can change positions. Examples of common verbal release cues include "break," "okay," and "free."

FOOD DRIVE

Teaching your dog how to work for his meals can be incredibly important when you want to build up food drive. I recommend that dog owners use their dog's meals to train throughout the day or during a designated training time. Teaching your dog how to work for food can be invaluable when training new skills.

Each day, select a time that is convenient for you to spend five minutes training. If you aren't able to train at your dog's mealtimes, take approximately half of his daily rations to store until you're ready.

Do what works for you! I find it easiest to put my dog's meal in his bowl, then take him to a quiet area to train. I will use about half to three-quarters of his food working and then put the rest down for him to eat.

Training every day can seem daunting! Take it one day at a time and do your best. You will find that once you start and get into a routine, it gets easier and is a whole lot of fun for both of you!

"GET IT!" GAME

Throwing a piece of food and having your dog go get it may appear silly, but it's actually one of the first ways to teach a dog to work for food.

Start out simple for the dog, throwing first to the left and then to the right. Say, "Get it!" and toss a piece of food. **A**

When he gets to the food and eats it, say "Get it!" and toss another piece in the other direction. **B**

You may need to do very short throws at first to make it easy for your dog. As he gets better at chasing down the food, you can toss it a bit further. You can work on this daily while teaching the game to your dog, and as he gets better at it, you can change it up and mix in some other fun behaviors. Keep your sessions short, using only a handful or two of kibble (or less, depending on your dog's size) while teaching your dog this game so that you maintain his interest. Using dry food is recommended.

IMPULSE CONTROL

Teaching impulse control while training with food is a great way to help your dog learn patience. It can help your dog be calm, show less frustration, or be less demanding when you ask him to wait for something he really wants.

Have your dog in a sit in front of you (page 37). If he has not yet learned to sit, you can lure him into position. Place some food on the ground and reward your dog for staying in a sit. **C**

The goal is to get your dog to sit and look at you, not at the food on the ground. **D**

This is difficult for some dogs, so you may need to use your hand to cover the food if he goes after it once you've placed it on the floor.

Wait for your dog to make eye contact with you, mark with a "yes!" and feed your dog a different piece of food from your hand. You do this to reward him for ignoring the food and making the decision to focus on you instead. Pick the food up, and start over. Practice this over several short sessions until it is easy for your dog to ignore the food on the ground.

The next step is to work on this at varying levels of difficulty. For example, drop the food instead of placing it on the ground, toss it close to your dog, or make it "roll" across the floor. **E**

Once your dog is able to ignore the food while he is sitting, you can have him in different positions, such as down or standing. When you change the dog's position, you are also increasing the difficulty, so you'll want to back up and start at the beginning and place the food rather than dropping, tossing, or rolling it.

LURING

Teaching your dog to follow a lure is relatively easy.

Take a piece of food, place it directly in front of your dog's nose, and slowly move it forward. As he steps toward it to follow, mark with a "yes!" and reward with the food you are using as the lure.

Repeat several times, increasing the distance your dog goes before marking and rewarding. Remember to keep the food close to his nose and go slowly at first.

Once your dog has the hang of going straight when being lured, try different directions to ensure he understands. You may need a few short sessions before your dog is comfortable following the lure in every direction.

USING TREATS

Using treats is something that I personally choose to do only in environments that are brand-new and/or extremely distracting. I have found that using the dog's food at home and saving the higher-value treats for training in unfamiliar areas is very effective. When a dog is food motivated, in some cases using extremely high-value food can cause the dog to be in a high state of arousal and he may become so focused on the food that it makes it difficult for him to learn new skills.

With that in mind, I believe new behaviors should always be taught in a familiar environment. Once we go to perform somewhere or I need the dog to be very focused, I will then use something of higher value. Each dog determines what high value is, but some common choices are cheese, steak, chicken, hot dogs, and freeze-dried liver.

TOY DRIVE

Being able to take your dog to the park and play a game of fetch sounds perfect! The only problem? Your dog doesn't come when called or even retrieve! Building up a dog's toy drive is a fantastic way to both create focus and help build a stronger bond between the two of you.

TEACHING TUG

Growing up, I was always told that playing tug with your dog would create aggression. This is absolutely not the case! Every game has rules, and the game of tug is no different! Teaching your dog the rules of the game is very important—being able to both start and end the game are key elements.

Using two rope toys or similar toys, run one of the toys along the ground and encourage your dog to chase it. **A**

Once he grabs the toy, pull back gently and then allow him to tug it away from you. Don't let go just yet—wait until he offers another tug. When he does, let go and allow him to win the toy. Throw a "mini party" (cheer him on, he won!) and then pull out the second toy and repeat the game. **B**

As he begins to understand the game, he will bring back the toy he just won to start playing again, rather than wait for you to pull out the second toy. Building up your dog's desire to tug will help with this confidence and gives the two of you a fun way to bond! **C**

TEACHING AN "OUT"

Ending a game of tug should be as easy as giving your dog a simple cue. I use the word "out" and teach this as a trick with a toy reward.

While your dog is tugging with you, stop moving and go completely still. **D**

If necessary, place your tug toy against your thighs to prevent any movement. When your dog releases the toy, mark with a "yes!" and reward the dog by starting up the game again. Keep practicing this over several short sessions until you're sure the dog will release the toy when you go still.

You can now give releasing the tug toy a cue. Stop moving, then just as the dog is about to let go, say "out!" When he lets go, mark with a "yes!" and throw the toy. **E**

This mixes up the game every once in a while and also allows for some breaks in between sessions.

TEACHING A SWITCH

To teach a switch, you'll need to use two toys, ideally of the same kind (i.e., two rope toys). Place one toy in your pocket (or behind your back) so your dog can't see it.

Start to play tug with the toy in your hands. **F**

When you're ready, pull out the toy from your pocket. When your dog sees it, start to make the toy "come alive" (move it around, get excited about it). **G**

Your dog should drop the toy he has and grab on to the toy you're currently playing with. Practice switching back and forth between both toys.

THE IMPORTANCE OF STRUCTURE

Structure is something that should be implemented the moment you bring your dog home. This can be as simple as creating a routine and doing your best to stick to it to help your dog develop good habits.

This will look different for each household. Think about what is important for your home, and then figure out what you need to do to get there. Being able to set very clear boundaries and have an effective way to communicate with your dog will help the two of you live together peacefully and have a lot of fun along the way.

Structure is not always at the top of the requirement list for new dog owners. However, implementing structure in your dog's life can take a lot of the pressure off the dog. When the human half of the team makes the majority of the decisions, while still providing proper enrichment and allowing the dog to make appropriate choices, many behavioral issues can be avoided.

This doesn't mean your dog can't just be a dog (every dog needs time to "dog"!), but it does give him a very clear understanding of what is expected and helps him learn from day one. It will help him relax, settle, and be what is known to the majority of people as a "good dog."

Structure (routine) is created by using place work to teach your dog how to settle, crate training to provide him with a safe space of his own, and daily exercise and mental stimulation—with some time set aside for fun and games too! Taking the time to train your dog will help the two of you have a clear line of communication and strengthen your bond.

PLACE WORK

Place work is teaching a dog to go to a designated area, usually a mat, raised platform, or cot, and remain there until you release him. Teaching a dog to do absolutely nothing is one of the most overlooked training skills. When a calm and structured environment is implemented, the dog naturally becomes much more focused, and training becomes easier.

Place work can be used for so many life experiences. It's a spot for your dog to be calm and relaxed. By giving your dog a job (lie down and relax), you are challenging his brain and providing him with great mental exercise. Practice place work on a daily basis and you should see positive changes start to show up in your dog's day-to-day life.

PLATFORM INTRODUCTION

Introducing your dog to an elevated platform, such as a cot, is a key element of place work training. It's very important to give your dog a positive association with a new object, as some dogs can be a little nervous with novelty items. However, with enough motivation, any dog can become confident enough to get onto a new surface.

Using food, lure your dog onto the elevated platform.

Be sure to mark and reward for each paw that is placed up on it. Once your dog places all four paws on the new surface, be sure to offer a jackpot for the behavior!

Continue to practice by luring your dog onto the platform. Be sure to use a hand gesture as you do so, such as a sweeping motion with your hand, beginning at the dog's nose and ending with your hand pointing at the platform. **A**

Once the dog is consistently offering the behavior of all four paws on the platform, you can start to ask your dog to lie down.

Practice this several times. Once your dog is beginning to lie down without any prompts from you, it is time to put a name to this behavior. I recommend "place" or "bed." **B**

DURATION

Duration can be one of the most difficult parts of teaching place work. Being able to put your dog on "place" and leave the room is only one aspect of this behavior. Teaching your dog to do nothing is essentially teaching him how to relax—and making that part of his job. Rewarding your dog for being relaxed and staying on place are two key elements to being successful with duration.

Use a leash at least 6 feet (2 m) in length to tether your dog. **C**

Attach the leash to his collar, then attach the other end to a solid object, such as a couch or heavy table. Practice moving around the room and go back to your dog to reward him for staying in position.

If your dog tries to get up or leave the platform, use the leash to gently guide him back into position. **D**

Try not to reward your dog with attention for getting up or leaving the platform. Using the leash helps to keep attention to a minimum, while at the same time providing light guidance when it is needed.

As you start working on duration, you can try reading, watching a movie, or making dinner while your dog is on the platform. The key is to frequently reward relaxed behavior, such as putting his head down, lying on his side, or starting to fall asleep. **E**

Once your dog has done well with the leash, you can remove it and start using a tab leash. This is a much shorter leash that allows you to give guidance as required.

DISTANCE

Distance can be challenging to achieve, but once your dog understands what you're asking for, he will show much more confidence with the platform.

Start by asking your dog to stay (page 13), go to the platform, and place a small amount of food on top. **F**

Go back to your dog and release him to go get the food. As he eats, ask him to lie down. Be sure to go back to him and reward if he follows through so he will be more inclined to continue to perform the behavior. **G**

If lying down is just a bit too much for your dog with the distance that's been added, try starting a little closer to the platform for the next attempt and work to increase distance from that point.

After several good sessions, try pretending to put food down on the platform. Continue this several times until your dog is consistently going to the platform and lying down. As your dog has more success and his confidence grows, be sure to start using the cue you've chosen for the behavior. At this point you can start increasing the distance between yourself and your dog's place, and you can even start asking your dog to go to his place from other rooms of the house. Be sure to reward his successes generously!

DOOR MANNERS

Door manners are such an important life skill for a dog. Using place work can help this skill become manageable and easy.

Using a doorbell or the sound of someone knocking on the door, start to pair the sound with the "place" behavior. Have someone ring the doorbell or knock on the door, give your place cue, and reward your dog when he gets on the platform. To make it as easy as possible for your dog, it's a good idea to stand very close to the platform when asking for the behavior and work back up to asking from a distance. **H**

Continue to practice this until your dog starts to offer to go to the platform when he hears the sound.

NOTE: *If you don't have a second person, you can use your phone to play the sound. I recommend using a Bluetooth speaker to be sure the sound is loud enough.*

CRATE TRAINING

Bringing a new puppy or dog into your home is exciting! One of the first things you may want to do is allow your new dog to sleep in bed with you. Co-sleeping is perfectly okay, but for people who prefer to keep the bed a human-only zone, using a crate provides your new dog with his own "bedroom." A crate may help prevent separation anxiety, gives the dog his own space, and helps create a consistent daily routine. Crate training can be used to help get your new dog through puppyhood, or it may be used throughout your dog's life.

SELECTING THE RIGHT CRATE FOR YOUR DOG

The size of your dog's crate is important and should be taken into account when purchasing one. You want the crate to be big enough to allow your dog to stand up, turn around, lie down, and stretch out comfortably. Choosing a crate that's the correct size can help discourage accidents for a lot of dogs.

There are different types of crates, and picking the right one will largely depend on what the crate will be used for. For a crate that will be put in the car, getting one that is crash tested for safety is generally something that should be considered. If the crate is just for the home, I recommend purchasing an airline-style crate.

These are easy to clean and are more like a den, which a fair number of dogs prefer. If your dog likes to be able to see his surroundings or feels more comfortable being able to see his people, there are also wire crates that would work and can easily be covered for those times when he needs a little solitude.

HOW I CRATE TRAIN

The following routine should be done while you are at home, many times throughout the day, using your dog's meals. Think of it like a game you'll play with your dog. I recommend increasing the amount of time your dog stays inside the crate slowly. Remember to go at your dog's pace to keep the game fun and to avoid unnecessary stress. Each step may take a few days and may need to be repeated multiple times.

Toss some of your dog's food into the crate and allow your dog to go inside to eat it and investigate. **A**

As he turns around to exit, reward again with some additional food inside the crate. **B**

Then allow him to walk out, making sure to remain calm. Repeat this process several times until your dog is going inside the crate without having to throw food into it.

At this point you can start asking your dog to lie down (page 38), rewarding him with food for doing this behavior inside the crate. **C**

If you have a brand-new puppy that hasn't yet learned to lie down on cue, you can lure your puppy's nose to the floor of the crate to help encourage him and then reward once he is in the desired position. When your dog is comfortable going inside the crate, toss some food inside after he enters and then close the door. **D**

Only keep the door closed very briefly, just long enough for him to finish eating, and then open the door and allow him to come out. Repeat this step, making sure he's happy while the door is closed.

As long as he is adapting well, instead of opening the door immediately once he's finished, you can start to feed him food through the door, keeping it closed and continuing to reward for him being inside. After feeding him a few pieces of kibble through the door, open it up, allowing him to come out, and continue to repeat this step as necessary.

SPECIAL CONSIDERATIONS

There are a few hurdles that can sometimes accompany crate training, especially for longer periods of time, such as overnight. For example, some dogs can be very vocal in the crate. There are several things you can do to help a new puppy decrease this behavior:

- The crate can be put in the bedroom with his people, next to the bed.

- A blanket that smells like his littermates is helpful if you received one; if not, a shirt that has your scent on it can be used instead.

- Make sure that he's been taken outside before asking him to settle. A puppy-safe chew, such as a KONG filled with some of his food, may help him relax as chewing is a very calming behavior.

For an older dog, it's important to ensure he doesn't think that barking or whining will get his human to open the crate door. Doing this may teach your dog that if he makes any amount of noise, he will be let out. It's best to wait until he has settled and is quiet to release him from the crate. If you are struggling with whining or barking, covering the crate can be a big help for dogs of any age, and I also recommend using white noise, such as a fan, or leaving the radio on.

If you need to crate your dog for a little bit longer than you normally would, it's a good idea to exercise your dog both mentally and physically beforehand. There are several different ways to accomplish this: a game of fetch, a nice long walk, and some trick training are all excellent options to help tire him out.

Keep in mind that crate training is a process. The more games you and your dog play, and the happier a place the crate is made out to be, the more comfortable your dog will become.

LEASH WALKING

Taking your dog out of the house shouldn't be a stressful or difficult thing to do! Teaching your dog how to walk properly on a leash without pulling will make those outings together much more enjoyable. When you genuinely enjoy spending time with your dog, you tend to do it more often, which is another great way to build on your relationship.

MATERIALS REQUIRED

- Food
- Slip leash

NOTE: *The placement of the slip leash is important in order to properly release pressure and not damage the dog's trachea. Proper positioning of the slip leash will be an important part of teaching the dog how to walk nicely. Use the tab on the leash to fit it around your dog's neck, behind his ears.* **A**

PRACTICE MAKES PERFECT

To begin, start in a very low-distraction environment. Indoors is best, where it is just you and the dog. With the leash in position and your dog at your side, take a few steps forward.

When your dog follows and the leash stays loose, mark with a "yes!" and reward. Be sure to reward right at your leg—it will encourage your dog to be in the correct position. **B**

Continue to practice over several short sessions, increasing the number of steps taken if your dog is staying with you.

Now change it up! Add in something your dog finds distracting (his favorite toy, for example) and see if he can maintain his loose leash. Mark with a "yes!" and reward if he can. Move the item to a less distracting place (further from you both) if he is having trouble. Try this with multiple items! **C**

Okay, time to change locations! Try this in different spots in your house, your yard, your driveway, etc. Reward your dog often for staying in position.

TAKING IT ON THE ROAD

Once your dog has success in many locations around the home, it's time to teach him how to walk nicely in public. It's important that he fully understands what you're asking of him before beginning to walk.

You may need to go back to taking only a few steps at a time. Make sure you reward your dog often for being in the correct position. The more often he is right, the more often he will want to be right, and the easier it will be for both of you.

If your dog does happen to tighten up his leash while walking, gently apply light pressure by stopping and bringing the leash back toward you in a quick motion (do not yank). Once you have gained your dog's attention and he has started to move toward you, mark with a "yes!" but no food. The reward should be continuing to walk forward as long as the leash remains loose. You can reward your dog with food whenever he returns to your side. **D**

TROUBLESHOOTING

If you're having trouble getting your dog's attention on a walk, he likely needs more practice in less distracting environments. Go back a step or two—practice some more in your yard, add in more distractions in a controlled environment, maybe enlist the help of a friend to add additional distractions. Keep it fun! Once inside the house has been mastered, you can try going further outside again.

ENVIRONMENTAL AND SOCIALIZATION TRAINING

It is incredibly important to socialize your dog from a young age, if possible. That said, if you never had the chance and adopted an older dog, it's still important to properly introduce him to the sights and sounds of the world. Everyone would like a dog that can be brought anywhere and has the ability to show off some of the fun tricks he has been taught! Working on socializing your dog will help him build up his confidence and become much more reliable in every situation.

START SLOW

New puppies or dogs should be introduced to different experiences slowly and with very few distractions. Going to an empty park with very little activity; playing different sounds on your phone at low volume, such as children yelling, storms, or alarms; or standing outside a store and people watching are some great low-key ways for early socialization.

TRAINING IN PUBLIC

Going to a dog park is not something I generally recommend. Dog parks can be filled with diseases, such as parvo, giardia, etc. Dogs that have not had all of their vaccinations are more at risk for some illnesses and there are often no regulations on what is required to visit a dog park. What's more, the activity that goes on in dog parks can encourage undesirable behaviors in your dog, such as excessive humping and bullying. Many people choose to use dog parks to give their dogs time to "be dogs." This is a nice idea, but it is actually a much better option to find a friend or neighbor that has a well-mannered, appropriately behaved dog that gets along well with others. This way, your dog can enjoy healthy, positive dog-dog interactions and learn good dog behavior.

Training in public, around other people, is another great way to help your dog's socialization. Take your dog's meal and try going to a local store that allows dogs. While there, you can practice tricks and obedience, or even just sit down and practice doing nothing, which is a skill all dogs should have.

Call ahead of time to make sure the store you want to visit will allow dogs. Some safe bets are businesses that don't serve food, such as home improvement stores, bookstores, outfitters, and, of course, pet stores (though you do run the risk of encountering poorly behaved dogs!).

If you live in an area with outdoor malls, these can be wonderful places to work with dogs. They offer a variety of new distractions and experiences for your dog, such as large groups of people, garbage cans, other leashed dogs in an open space, clothing racks, etc.

SUPER SIMPLE TRICKS

These tricks are cute and fun, and working on them before the tricks in some of the other chapters will engage your dog's brain. These tricks help develop the fundamental skills needed to begin the learning process. Essentially, they will help your dog "learn how to learn" and make teaching the more difficult tricks much easier and more enjoyable. The following behaviors are relatively simple, but many are the building blocks for the more complicated, flashy tricks later on!

Some of the tricks in this chapter also improve your dog's body awareness and balance, which are important and will be instrumental in learning some of the more difficult behaviors. Both balance and body awareness are key elements in many tricks and can also help prevent unwanted injuries.

Remember, easy doesn't mean boring! A lot of these tricks are party favorites, and they can be a great way to showcase your dog's talents.

SIT

This is often the first trick that people teach a dog—and for good reason! There are only a few steps, making it great to start with. Plus, sit is a building block that can be used for all sorts of more complex tricks (pages 85 to 131).

INSTRUCTIONS

While your dog stands in front of you, place a piece of food at his nose and move your hand up over his head and back so that he lifts his nose to follow it. **A** Lifting his head will cause his back end to drop to the floor. **B**

As soon as he gets into position, mark the behavior with a "yes" and release the food from your hand.

Repeat this several times. Take a break. Then continue to practice in short, two- to three-minute sessions.

Once your dog is consistently sitting, you can say "sit" just as he's getting into position. After a few repetitions, try cuing "sit" without the lure. **C** If he sits, give him a jackpot! If not, add the lure back in, but try again without the lure after one or two attempts.

Continue to practice until your dog sits every time he's cued.

TROUBLESHOOTING

If the dog is not sitting while being lured, it is often due to incorrect hand position. When you're having the dog follow the food, make sure your hand goes back in an arc and stays close to his nose.

DOWN

Like sit, down is a fundamental trick that is often taught early. I think it's a great idea to teach down as soon as possible, since it's useful on a daily basis. Dogs in the down position are often much more relaxed, as it is a behavior used for settling. Also, if your dog is out with you and needs to wait, it is handy for your dog to be able to lie down, as it is a much more natural and comfortable position than sitting. Keep your training sessions short for this one, just a few minutes in length, to keep it fun and interesting for the dog. You always want to end your training session while your dog is still engaged and wanting more!

INSTRUCTIONS

Hold a piece of food to your dog's nose, and have him follow it toward his chest and then straight to the floor. **A**

As soon as your dog has dropped into position, mark with a "yes!" and reward. **B**

When your dog is easily lying down while being lured, you can cue "down" just as he's getting into position. Repeat this step several times.

Try cuing "down" without luring. If your dog lies down, give him a jackpot! If not, continue to lure him, but after another few attempts, make sure to try again without the food lure.

Keep practicing in short two- to three-minute sessions until your dog is performing the "down" behavior on cue.

TIP: *While your dog is lying down, feeding a few extra pieces of food can help encourage him to stay in position.*

TROUBLESHOOTING

If your dog stands up while being lured or seems to have a hard time fully lying down, I recommend you work on luring him under your leg, a chair, or a coffee table—this will require him to crouch and increases the chance of the behavior occurring.

You can also try placing the dog up on an elevated surface, such as a couch or platform. Place the food at his nose, and slowly lure him down, bringing your hand below the surface level of where you've placed your dog.

It's very important to reward even the smallest attempts to lie down if your dog is having trouble. Elbows bending closer to the floor, or his chest or head dropping down low, are examples of what to look for and reward.

Remember, when your dog needs extra help, rewarding small steps toward your end goal will help your dog have the most success!

ROLL OVER

This trick is one many people want to teach a new dog because it looks adorable, it's quick moving, and it's a lot of fun to show off. It requires a fair amount of trust between the dog and handler, as a dog often feels vulnerable exposing his belly, so you may need to spend a bit of extra time on each step and provide some extra encouragement. Don't be discouraged! Some dogs may roll right over, while others require a slower introduction. It's a trick that can really strengthen the bond between an owner and dog, so the finished behavior can provide a real sense of accomplishment.

INSTRUCTIONS

Start with your dog lying down in front of you. **A**

Take a piece of food and place it directly in front of his nose.

Lure his nose slowly around to his shoulder blade. **B**

This motion should cause him to shift his weight and lie on his side. Mark with a "yes!" and reward. Repeat until your dog is easily rolling onto his side. **C**

To encourage him to roll over completely, once you've lured your dog's nose to his shoulder blade, continue in the downward motion toward his spine, which will cause him to roll onto his back, then simply lure his nose in the direction you need him to go to roll onto his other side. **D**

Once he is following the lure all the way over easily, use your cue word, then lure him around. Repeat this several times, then try it without the food, using only your arm gesture to assist him. Mark with a "yes!" and give him a jackpot as he completes the behavior.

TROUBLESHOOTING

Test out both directions. Most dogs tend to prefer one side to the other. If your dog is struggling, sometimes switching to his other side can really help.

WAVE

This is one of my favorite tricks to teach. I think you'll find it's an absolutely perfect behavior to use for photos you take of your dog. And it can also be used as a cute party trick when guests arrive or leave! To start this trick, it's helpful if your dog knows how to shake a paw (page 49), but it isn't a requirement. If your dog does know how to shake, it will help you get to the final result a bit faster.

INSTRUCTIONS

Start with your dog sitting in front of you, and present your hand in a high-five position, but lower to the ground than you normally would. **A**

Take a piece of food, lure your dog's head up, and if your dog tries to offer a paw, mark with a "yes!" and reward. **B** Repeat a few times and then, when he is able to paw at your hand, raise it up a few inches higher. **C**

Repeat this step until you have your hand at the dog's eye level. When he can paw at your hand at that height, move your hand away as he goes to touch it, and reward. **D**

The hardest part of this trick is building the duration of the wave. Just be patient and don't rush! Taking your time and building up your dog's muscle memory is important and will help with the trick in the long run.

SPIN

Not only is a spinning dog adorable, spinning is also a trick that teaches a great body-awareness skill. Mastering this trick and teaching your dog how to turn in a complete circle will help him with rear-end awareness. It will also teach him how to move his body in a new way.

INSTRUCTIONS

It's best to start working on this trick while your dog is standing. If your dog keeps sitting or lying down while working, try moving around to help encourage your dog to stay standing.

Using food, lure your dog's head toward his hip, making sure to go slowly, and keep the food directly in front of his nose. **A** Mark the completed circle with a "yes" and release the food from your hand to reward.

Once your dog is following the lure all the way around easily, use your cue word, then lure him around. Repeat this several times, then try it without the food, using only your arm gesture to assist him. Mark with a "yes!" and give him a jackpot as he completes the behavior.

You can practice both sides, but I recommend getting your dog comfortable with one side at a time. **B**

TIP: *Remember, you don't want to start naming a trick until your dog is performing it consistently.*

SHAKE A PAW

When you bring a new dog into your home, you may think that teaching him to shake a paw will be adorable—and it is! However, I recommend teaching it after your dog has learned a few other behaviors, as it can encourage some dogs to offer a paw all the time.

Building on this trick, you can have your dog learn how to use his two front paws separately by giving each paw a different name!

BEFORE YOU BEGIN

Working on shake a paw requires your dog to already know how to sit (page 37) on cue.

INSTRUCTIONS

Have your dog sit in front of you and present one of your hands to him. **A** Wait a few seconds to see if he will lift one of his paws up.

If he does not, gently reach down with your hand to touch his paw, and when he lifts it off the ground, place your hand under it. **B** Mark with a "yes" and reward up high, at your dog's eye level. Repeat this step a few times.

Present your hand again without any prompting and wait to see if he offers his paw. If he does, mark and reward. **C**

Once he is consistently placing his paw in your hand when you offer it, give this trick a name (cue) and practice using the cue word.

TROUBLESHOOTING

If your dog doesn't like his paws touched, you'll want to work on making it a positive experience for him. Using his meal is an easy way to get in a training session. Lightly touch one of his paws, and feed him a few pieces of food. Repeat several times with each paw.

TAKE A BOW

While this is a fairly easy trick to teach, a word of warning: be careful what name you choose for it! In most cases, this trick is called "bow" because the dog looks like he is taking a bow. The biggest problem is that "bow" sounds very similar to "down" and it can be a bit confusing for the dog.

I highly recommend calling this trick something easier. A few of my favorites are "take a bow," "curtsy," "ta da," or "yoga." For my Super Collies, I like to use "finish," as I normally have them perform this behavior at the end of a routine.

INSTRUCTIONS

Start by luring your dog's nose to his chest. **A** You can accomplish this by placing your treat hand at the dog's nose and gently pushing your hand down and forward at a forty-five-degree angle (toward the middle of the dog's front legs). When your dog starts to bend his elbows, be sure to mark with a "yes" and then bring your food hand away from your dog to reward. **B** This prevents the dog from lying down.

Keep practicing, and reward as your dog's elbows get closer to the floor. Take this process slowly to be sure that you have lots of success. When the dog reaches the point where his elbows are touching the floor, start to wait a little longer before rewarding to build up duration in the position. Continue to mark and reward for a solid "bow!" **C**

TROUBLESHOOTING

If your dog is having trouble with this trick and his back end continuously drops down to the ground, help him out by placing your arm underneath his belly to prevent this from happening.

FOOTSIES

This trick reminds me of dancing on my father's feet when I was a little girl. It is a behavior that goes by several names, sometimes called "cop cop," "paws," or "feet." People tend to think this trick is very difficult because it looks impressive, but it can be accomplished easily in a few simple steps. It's a crowd-pleaser!

INSTRUCTIONS

This trick needs to be broken down into two separate parts in order to achieve success. Part one is teaching your dog to walk comfortably between your legs. **A**

Start off with your dog behind you. **B** Use food to lure him in between your legs and reward. Repeat this step several times until he is comfortable in the position.

Take a few steps forward, luring your dog to follow while in between your legs. **C** Then take a few steps backward. Reward him for staying in position. Repeat until your dog easily follows the food and stays with you.

When your dog can follow your movements without any issues, you can start part two.

Stand with your toes pointing toward each other and lure your dog in between your legs. **D** Once in position, use food and lure him forward slowly until one of his paws lands on your foot. **E** Mark with a "yes!" and reward. Continue with this step until you successfully get both paws on your feet.

Start to shift your weight lightly from side to side and reward your dog for staying on your feet.

The final step is to begin to walk forward. Do this slowly, rewarding each step at first, then every few steps. If your dog removes either paw from your feet, restart and keep practicing!

Keep your sessions short, two to three minutes in length.

TROUBLESHOOTING

If your dog has trouble placing his paws on your feet, try using larger shoes or a bowl. You can also work with the shoes independently and get your dog comfortable stepping on them. Place a bowl or shoes in front of you and have your dog step on it.

You can also ask for a "shake a paw" if your dog knows that behavior and allow his paw to land on the shoe to help jump-start the trick.

NOSE TOUCH

This is a great foundational skill I feel is often overlooked. Teaching your dog to target your hand with his nose can be used for so many things, such as standing still for handling, leading him where you need him to go, and gaining and maintaining focus.

For this trick we will use a training method called shaping. The key is to allow your dog to think on his own and reward him for making the right decision.

INSTRUCTIONS

Hold out the palm of your hand about 6 inches (15 cm) away from your dog **A** and wait for him to touch his nose to it. It may be a very light touch at first, so be sure to mark his effort with a "yes!" and reward.

As you practice and your dog is consistently pressing his nose to your hand, wait a second or two longer before you mark and reward to help build duration. **B**

Once your dog is actively pressing his nose to your hand and holding it there, add a verbal cue.

TROUBLESHOOTING

There are a few different things you can try if your dog is having difficulty:

- Move your hand closer to your dog. The less distance he has to go to touch your hand, the easier it will be for him.

- Rub some yummy-smelling food on your hand and then present your hand to your dog. The smell should entice him to nose your palm.

- Still didn't work? Try presenting your hand and wiggling your fingers. This should draw your dog's attention to your hand and encourage him to move toward it, giving you the opportunity to jump-start the behavior.

LEG WEAVES

This is a very fun, fast-moving trick used in a lot of canine freestyle routines (for more on freestyle, see page 161). Teaching your dog to weave between your legs is a very entertaining and engaging trick for both of you. It requires good timing and coordination from both the human and the dog to make this trick work, and when it all comes together, this fairly easy trick looks impressive!

INSTRUCTIONS

Start with your dog on your left side, either standing or in a sit. **A** Step forward with your right leg and, using food in your right hand, lure your dog under your leg. **B**

As your dog gets about halfway through your leg and starts to exit, be sure to mark with a "yes" and reward with the food from your hand after he has completely passed under your leg. Do this several times until your dog is very comfortable with the motion. **C**

Repeat this step on the other side, using your other hand to lure and reward.

Once your dog is easily going through your legs from both sides, you can start to take multiple steps. Hold food in each hand. Lure your dog under one leg, and instead of rewarding, lure him through the other leg, then give him a jackpot! **D**

Start to take multiple steps now, slowly luring your dog through each step. Reward every few steps.

Next, try taking a step and have your dog go through your leg without a food lure—simply use a finger to guide him through, and then reward.

Continue to use your finger, pointing to guide him through multiple leg weaves. Make sure to reward him every few steps. **E**

Keep practicing this step for several short sessions. Once your dog does this on a hand cue, you can name this behavior with a verbal cue and practice taking more steps forward.

TROUBLESHOOTING

If your dog is uneasy going through your legs, spend some time rewarding small steps. For example, if he can get his head through, mark and reward that.

Reward placement can also really help. If your dog backs up rather than completing the motion of going through your legs, try gently tossing the food out to the side to encourage him to go through completely.

BACKWARD LEG WEAVES

This is a fun trick to complete. It looks flashy but is relatively easy for the dog, especially if he has already mastered forward leg weaves. Having forward leg weaves (page 59) in your repertoire isn't a requirement before starting this trick, but it will make it much easier for both of you to complete. More often than not, it's the human half of the training team that has trouble with this one!

INSTRUCTIONS

Start with your dog in a sit in front of you. Take a step to the right with both feet, so your dog is now facing you, but off to your left. **A**

Take a step back with your right leg. **B** Place your right hand through your legs and lure your dog around the outside of your left leg and through toward your right side. **C**

Mark with a "yes" as he goes through your legs, and extend your right arm straight back behind you slightly to reward, so you are rewarding him in the direction you want him to go.

Repeat this step several times, then try adding one step at a time until you can take several steps backward. **D**

TIP: *Reward placement will play an important role with this trick. Rewarding him behind you teaches the dog the direction you would like him to go and sets him up for success.*

SIT PRETTY

This trick is perfect for building strength in your dog's core. In fact, due to the amount of strength required to perform this trick successfully, it tends to take a little longer to perfect. Don't be discouraged! Once your dog is easily sitting straight up, it's an amazing pose for pictures and is always fun to show off.

BEFORE YOU BEGIN

Working on sit pretty requires your dog to already know how to sit (page 37) on cue.

INSTRUCTIONS

Start with your dog in a sit. **A** Place a piece of food at your dog's nose and slowly bring the lure upward. **B** When his front paws come up off the ground, mark with a "yes!" and reward. This step will need to be repeated many times over short sessions, and as you progress, he should become steadier on his hind legs. **C**

As you progress with this trick, start to build duration by extending the time your dog holds his paws up before marking and rewarding the behavior.

When you are confident that your dog will easily get into position, add a cue!

TROUBLESHOOTING

The most important thing to remember with this trick is to take your time.

If your dog is having trouble getting his balance, try having him sit against a couch or other object. You can also stand behind the dog and use your legs as a way to help your dog balance while luring him up.

OVER ARMS

This trick is always fun, both to teach and to perform. Dogs love to jump . . . pair that with being able to jump around and over his owner, and your dog will be in heaven! As an added bonus, you'll not only exercise your dog's mind but also provide a fair amount of physical activity. Teaching your dog to jump over your arms in a circle is not only flashy-looking but also a great trick to add to a canine freestyle routine.

INSTRUCTIONS

Start facing a wall and have your dog off to either side. **A** Ask your dog to stay, place the palm of your hand low on the wall, and set a piece of food on the floor on the side opposite your dog. **B** You can also place your hand against another flat object, such as a cot on its side.

When you're ready, cue your dog to go get the food. Be sure your arm is low enough to encourage your dog to go over your arm rather than under it. **C** He may simply walk over your arm. This is absolutely fine to start but encourage him to jump as you progress.

Make sure you practice with both arms, so your dog is going over your arms from in front of you as well as from behind you.

Gradually raise your arm up a few inches at a time as your dog is successful at each new height.

Now begin to back away from the wall and allow a gap between your hand and the wall. **D** Repeat the previous steps but pretend to put food down. When your dog successfully jumps over your arm, mark with a "yes!" and reward.

The final step is to have your dog sit in front of you. Have food in both hands. Start with your right arm out to the side. **E** Cue your dog to jump over your right arm, using your left hand to lure him over if necessary.

As soon as he jumps over, bring your right arm around in front of you, put your left arm out to the side, and use your right hand to lure your dog over your left arm from behind you. **F** Practice this several times until your dog is successfully jumping over each arm without much assistance.

GO AROUND

Teaching your dog to go around your body is not only a fun trick but also a useful skill. For example, it's nice to have a dog that knows how to "go around" to get by an obstacle while out walking. It's also fun to be able to point to almost any object and send your dog around it! There are only a few steps to this trick, so with just a bit of practice you'll have a dog that can confidently run around you on cue and be set up to take part in other activities!

INSTRUCTIONS

Start with your dog standing in front of you. **A**

Make sure you have food in both hands. Using your right hand, lure your dog around behind your body. **B** Switch to your left hand to continue luring.

Mark with a "yes!" as he approaches the left side, and reward with your left hand once he arrives at that side. Repeat this step multiple times. **C**

Once your dog is fluently following your hands around your body with a lure, try it with just your hand guiding him around. **D**

Mark and reward with a jackpot if he is successful! If he still needs help, add the lure back in for a few more attempts, then try again.

Once your dog no longer requires the lure, you can name the behavior and help him out with a hand gesture as necessary.

TROUBLESHOOTING

If it is too big of a step going from two lures to none, try starting your dog out with a hand gesture and luring with your left hand only to help him with the last half of the trick.

BACK UP

Teaching a dog to back up is a great way to help him develop rear-end awareness. I recommend using two different types of flooring, such as hardwood and carpet, when beginning to teach this trick. The difference in flooring will help teach the dog that he should continue to back up until his back paws touch a specific spot. In most cases, the dog will usually start to offer the behavior after only a few sessions. I love teaching this trick—watching the dog figure it out is always rewarding.

INSTRUCTIONS

Start with your dog standing on surface I (hardwood or tile). **A**

Surface B (carpet or mat) should be just a few inches behind the dog's back paws.

Take a piece of food in your hand and gently push it toward your dog's chest.

This will cause him to take a step back so he can follow the food. As he backs up, he will step onto surface (carpet or mat). As soon as one of his back paws touches the carpet, mark with a "yes!" and reward. Practice this step several times. **B**

After a few sessions, instead of applying light pressure and encouraging your dog to step backward, give him the opportunity to back up onto the other surface on his own. Mark and reward when he offers the behavior. **C**

Increase the distance between the two surfaces by a few inches and keep practicing. Continue to add to the distance your dog has to travel backward to reach the carpet.

Start to name the trick with your verbal cue once your dog is offering it consistently!

TROUBLESHOOTING

Some dogs pick up behaviors more quickly than others. If your dog has trouble with the "back-up" behavior, decrease the distance he has to travel to reach the carpet/mat and try again.

JUMP IN ARMS

This trick is very popular in the dog sport world, as it can be used at the end of a successful dog sport competition or as a flashy move in a freestyle routine. However, it can also be useful if you need to carry your dog somewhere but he's the type of dog that dislikes being picked up. Note that this trick works best when performed with a dog under 50 pounds (23 kg), as it requires you to be strong enough to catch him!

INSTRUCTIONS

Start by sitting in a chair that does not have any armrests. **A**

Have your dog sit off to your side and lure him up onto your lap. At first your dog will probably crawl onto your lap. This is acceptable to begin with, but after several successful repetitions, try to ask for a bit more. **B**

As a next step, place your dog a little further away from you. Ask him to jump onto your lap using your food lure, and reward if he does. **C**

If he's still having trouble, remove yourself from the chair and practice luring your dog up onto it when it's empty. **D**

Once your dog is jumping up onto your lap successfully, it's time to move on to the next step!

Find a wall that you can lean against, and create a "chair" with your legs. Practice getting your dog to jump up onto your bent legs. **E**

Start to stand up, working in stages to gradually straighten your legs—how fast you are able to straighten your legs will depend on the individual dog. **F**

I always recommend that once standing, you present one bent leg and get your dog to jump up onto that. This will also help with a heavier dog, since he will jump on your leg and then you can lift him into your arms the rest of the way.

As your dog gets better at this skill, you can practice only presenting your arms and cuing your dog to jump into them! **G**

TROUBLESHOOTING

If your dog is having problems jumping into your lap or even onto the chair, try using something lower, such as an ottoman.

SAY YOUR PRAYERS

This trick is one of the most adorable ones to show off, and it's always a hit with crowds, big or small. It's rather amusing to have your dog "pray" before he eats a meal or gets into bed, and it can be cute to have your dog perform a variation of the trick (for example, paws on a stool instead of your arm) while you set down his food bowl, rather than simply having him sit while waiting.

There are two parts to get to the final behavior. The size of your dog will determine whether you use your arm or your leg as a prop. A smaller dog does best with an arm, and for a larger dog, it's much easier to use your leg to support him.

INSTRUCTIONS

Step one is to teach your dog to put his paws up on your arm or leg.

Start with your dog in a sit. **A**

Place the lure at his nose and pull it slowly forward, over your arm or leg in an upward motion to encourage him to place his paws up on you. **B**

Repeat several times over short sessions until you can present your arm or leg, and your dog will place both paws up.

Next, if you are using your left side for your dog's paws, take food in your right hand and place it under your left arm or leg, in between you and your dog. **C**

Lure your dog's nose down in between his paws, and mark with a "yes!" and reward your dog for staying in this position.

Nearly every dog will drop one paw at this point. Keep practicing and be sure to reward your dog only if both paws remain on your arm or leg. This step can take some practice, so take your time.

Once he is successfully putting his face between his paws, you can name the behavior and practice using the verbal cue. Rewarding your dog multiple times while he is in the position will help you gain duration. **D**

CRAWL

Teaching your dog to crawl is a fun party trick. It is also a behavior that will help build up your dog's core strength and joint flexibility, while at the same time provide a mini workout for your dog. Consider the surface you're asking your dog to crawl on—he will be much more likely to perform this behavior on a soft surface, such as carpet.

BEFORE YOU BEGIN

Working on crawl will require your dog to already know how to lie down (page 38) on cue.

INSTRUCTIONS

Start with your dog lying down in front of you. **A**

Hold food between your thumb and finger directly in front of your dog's nose.

Have him follow the food close to floor level, then lure him toward you. When he starts to shuffle forward toward you, mark with a "yes" and reward. Repeat several times. **B**

Increase the amount of forward movement you require gradually, one shuffle at a time, to keep success rates high.

Practice this several times in short sessions (just a few minutes in length) until your dog is successfully crawling forward.

Start to build even more duration by luring him forward while you back up.

At this point, when your dog understands what you're asking for, you can add your cue. Do a few repetitions with the food lure, then try it without!

TROUBLESHOOTING

Some dogs automatically stand up when doing any forward movement. To help your dog stay close to floor level, you can lure him lengthwise under a coffee table. This requires him to stay low to move forward.

If he is uncertain about being under such a large object for any length of time, try a shorter object, like a chair or a broom handle—anything that will require him to get down low and move forward to get the food will give you the opportunity to reward forward motion close to the ground.

SUPER IMPRESSIVE TRICKS

Once your dog has learned several basic tricks, you can build on them to start performing more complex ones. These tricks are the "next step" in training your dog. I think you'll find that working together to achieve them will help you have a happier and healthier bond, as well as build up your dog's confidence in himself and his ability to learn.

CROSS YOUR PAWS

There's always going to be that one trick that seems impossible to achieve, and for many dogs, "cross your paws" is that trick. Hero was the first dog I taught this behavior to; using an older method than the one I share here, it took years for him to master it! Since this is a commonly used trick in canine freestyle and is also a fun pose to use for photos, I needed an easier way for my other dogs to learn, but every book and video I watched used the same method I had used with Hero.

The steps I use to teach this trick now are different, yet very simple. Every Super Collie since Hero has learned this trick easily and in a very short amount of time! Still, be patient as you teach your dog this trick.

BEFORE YOU BEGIN

Working on cross your paws requires your dog to already know how to lie down (page 38) on cue.

INSTRUCTIONS

Have your dog lie down in front of you. **A**

Cover one of your dog's front paws with your hand. **B**

If your dog doesn't appreciate having his paws touched, spend some time touching each one and rewarding your dog so he develops a positive association with paw handling.

Using food, lure your dog's nose over the paw that you have covered. **C**

Do this very slowly and mark with a "yes" when your dog moves his other paw over the covered one. Reward and repeat this several times. If your dog seems to have trouble crossing one paw over the other, try working from the other side instead—every dog has a paw preference!

As you practice, you can remove your hand from your dog's paw and continue to lure his nose over the paw that was previously covered. Slowly move your hand holding the food further away from your dog's face, marking and rewarding each time he crosses one paw over the other. **D**

Only name the trick and begin using your cue once your dog is completing it almost every time.

Once your dog has mastered one side, start working on the other side as well. Keep in mind that every dog has an easier time with one paw than the other, so it may be more difficult to teach the other side. **E**

HIDE IN SUITCASE

The most ridiculous dog trick that I have ever taught is this one—and of course it was the one that went viral when I put it up on social media. I honestly didn't think anything of the trick when I posted it, but the video of Hero running into a suitcase received over 20 million views within the first few days of being online. It is definitely a crowd favorite now!

MATERIALS REQUIRED

• Suitcase

NOTE: *For this trick, using a soft-sided fabric suitcase that is an appropriate size for your dog will be an important factor in your dog's success.*

INSTRUCTIONS

To increase your dog's comfort, start with the suitcase open, place your dog inside, and feed him inside the suitcase. **A**

Some dogs take longer than others with this trick, because being inside a suitcase is a completely new experience. Take your time, and if your dog is a little nervous, I recommend taking a few days to allow him to acclimate.

A

Once your dog is comfortable with the suitcase, begin having him jump in and out of the suitcase, using a small, sweeping hand gesture to guide him. The gesture should start from just in front of where the dog is standing and head toward the suitcase. If necessary, you can use a piece of food to lure him a few times. **B**

When he is comfortable getting in and out, take the suitcase lid and hold it partially closed. Again, have him work on getting in and out of the suitcase. **C**

Once your dog is getting in and out of the suitcase easily, start asking him to lie down inside of it. Close the suitcase lid, open it back up immediately, and reward. Repeat this several times. **D**

The next step is to get the dog to "open" the suitcase lid. The secret here is to zip up a portion of the suitcase so that the lip is angled, making it much easier for the dog to open. **E** Start by putting food inside the suitcase and asking your dog to get it. When he nudges the corner of the suitcase, be sure to mark with a "yes" and reward. Repeat this several times until your dog nudges the suitcase open and gets the food located inside.

The final step is to stop putting food inside the suitcase and work on putting the whole behavior together. This will take patience—just be sure to mark and reward all the dog's efforts at first, and then selectively reward for better and better responses. **F**

TURN LIGHTS ON AND OFF

This trick is incredibly fun to teach and has practical applications as well. If a human companion needs assistance turning lights on and off, it is incredibly helpful if a dog is able to perform that task. I always recommend focusing on one part at a time and never teaching them together. If you have a smaller dog that cannot reach a light switch, you can use a floor lamp that has a switch on the base, or you can get creative and have a small staircase or platform the dog can stand on to reach a particular switch.

MATERIALS REQUIRED

- Pen cap
- Tape

INSTRUCTIONS

TURNING LIGHTS ON

Attach a pen cap to the light switch. Use a piece of tape to ensure it stays secure. This will expedite training and give your dog a larger target to work with.

Take a piece of food and lure your dog's nose to the bottom of the pen cap, then lure upward so that his nose hits it. **A**

His nose hitting the cap up should turn on the light, so when it does, mark with a "yes!" and reward. Repeat this step several times over several short sessions.

Next, try to lure your dog with just your hand. Mark and reward if he turns on the light. Practice this several times, then attempt to wait and see if he will nudge the pen cap on his own. If he does, mark and give him a jackpot!

The next step is to remove the pen cap. Add your lure back in temporarily if necessary, but very quickly (within a few repetitions) have him try to turn on the lights without being lured. You can now name the behavior. **B**

Practice with your verbal cue until your dog is confidently turning on the lights when cued to do so.

TURNING LIGHTS OFF

Place the pen cap back on the light switch.

Take a piece of food and lure your dog's nose from the top of the pen cap and down so that his nose hits the cap and turns off the light. **C**

Mark with a "yes!" and reward. Repeat this step several times, over several short sessions as necessary.

Once he is easily tapping the pen cap down with his nose, try to lure him with just your hand. Mark and reward if he turns the light off. **D**

Continue to practice this several times, then wait to see if he will nudge the pen cap on his own. If he does, mark and give him a jackpot!

The next step is to remove the pen cap. Add your lure back in temporarily if necessary, but very quickly (within a few repetitions) have him try to turn off the lights without being lured. You can now name the behavior.

Practice with your verbal cue until your dog is confidently turning off the lights when given the cue.

PUTTING IT ALL TOGETHER

When I first start to practice on and off together, I always use my hand as a guide with the cue for the dog. Lure upward for on and downward for off in order to help him out. You can fade out your hand as soon as your dog is comfortable performing both together.

SELFIE

If you only teach your dog one trick from this chapter, I'd probably recommend this one. Being able to have your dog take a selfie with you not only looks adorable but also makes for the best photos (to share and to have framed)! This trick may look difficult, but it really is easier than you think for your dog to learn.

BEFORE YOU BEGIN

Working on a selfie requires your dog to already know how to sit (page 37) on cue.

INSTRUCTIONS

Start by having your dog in a sit behind you. **A**

Place a piece of food in one of your hands and lure him up onto your shoulders. **B** At first he may place both paws on the same shoulder. **C**

I highly recommend using food and luring your dog over to the opposite shoulder—he will move one paw at a time, so when you feel one paw on each shoulder, mark with a "yes!" and reward. **D**

The timing of the reward is important—make sure you reward him when his head is over one of your shoulders. Repeat this step over several short sessions.

Once your dog has mastered placing one paw on each shoulder, add the cue word you've chosen, such as "selfie." Say your cue, then lure your dog up onto your shoulders. Mark with a "yes!" and reward. Practice this several times, then try cuing your dog without the lure. When he puts his paws up, mark and give him a jackpot!

Keep practicing until your dog can be given the cue from in front of you. This may take several attempts over a few sessions but keep at it and you'll soon have an adorable pose for pictures of the two of you!

TROUBLESHOOTING

Reward placement is important with this trick. When you are luring your dog so that one paw is placed on each shoulder, make sure you keep the food close to your head to encourage him to move one paw to the opposite shoulder and not drop both paws to the ground.

ORBIT

Teaching your dog to walk backward around an object (or you!) is a flashy dog trick. By working on this trick, you also introduce your dog to rear-end awareness, which is a must-have for many different tricks, including rebounding, different types of jumps for disc, or any type of balancing trick. It can also help your dog avoid injuries, so this is something I would teach any dog!

MATERIALS REQUIRED

- Medium-size dog food bowl (must have a wide, flat bottom)

INSTRUCTIONS

Start with a medium-size dog food bowl. Flip it over so that the flat bottom is facing up.

Lure your dog's two front paws onto the surface of the dog bowl.

Mark with a "yes!" and reward when he gets both paws up. Repeat this step several times over several short sessions until your dog is easily putting his paws up on the bowl. **A**

A

TROUBLESHOOTING

If your dog has trouble with the first step, you can put the bowl between your feet and lure your dog in between your legs and onto it. Reward for any paw touching the top of the bowl. Once your dog is comfortable putting both paws up, you can remove yourself and lure your dog's front two paws onto the bowl.

If your dog has trouble keeping his front paws up on the bowl while moving his back paws, try using a larger bowl with more surface area. Work your way up to using a medium-size bowl. Reward for every small step made by the back paws.

The next step is adding movement! Have your dog place his paws up onto the bowl. Put food to his nose, and gently walk into him. As your dog takes a step away from you and to the side, mark with a "yes!" and reward. **B** You want to reward for any movement of his back paws as long as his front paws stay on the bowl.

As you practice and your dog starts moving around the bowl, you can slowly remove yourself. **C** Lure him around and see if he moves without you helping by walking with him. If he can move without you, mark with a "yes!" and give him a jackpot. Have him take multiple steps without you. If he gets stuck, help him out.

The last step is to move your dog around the bowl entirely without you.

This could be very slow at first, but as your dog progresses, he should get faster and it should become much easier. Once he is able to spin around the bowl easily, you can name the behavior and transfer it to other objects with your verbal cue, including yourself!

Transferring this trick to yourself is easy! Have food in both hands and start your dog on the side of you that he is most comfortable on. Start by luring him, back end first, around the back of your body. Once he is close to the other side of you, switch hands and continue around your body.

When your dog is easily going around you, and you have practiced many times, you will be able to lure less and eventually just use a hand gesture to encourage your dog around you.

SHY

This is one of the most popular tricks shared on social media, and for good reason: teaching your dog to cover his eyes makes for some great photos and can make anyone smile. This behavior requires some patience to complete though. The biggest tip I can give is to have your dog in a sit. If you start with your dog in a down, it may turn into the default position for this trick, which will make teaching it in other positions a little more difficult in the future. If your dog lies down, simply stop and reposition him.

MATERIALS REQUIRED

You'll need something to place on your dog's nose/snout, such as tape, a small sticky note, or a hair elastic.

BEFORE YOU BEGIN

Working on shy requires your dog to already know how to sit (page 37) on cue.

INSTRUCTIONS

Start with your dog in a sit in front of you. Place the tape or sticky note on his nose, or the hair elastic around his muzzle. **A** When he lifts his paw to swipe at his face, mark with a "yes!" and reward. In some cases, you may need to wait for a bit for your dog to lift his paw up to his face.

Repeat this step several times over short sessions.

You now need to decide which paw you would prefer your dog to use. I recommend selecting the one your dog is choosing to use the majority of the time, and then only reward him when he uses the paw you've chosen.

Fading out the tape or hair elastic is the next step. To do this, remove it and very lightly tap your dog's nose. **B** When you do this, he should use his paw to swipe at his face, as he has been previously rewarded for doing this behavior when he feels something touch his nose or muzzle. Continue to mark and reward the desired behavior.

Once you can lightly tap and your dog immediately swipes at his face, you can add a cue, such as "shy," "cover," or "bashful." **C**

FOOTSTALL

The footstall is one of the most popular stunt dog tricks you will see if you attend a dog show. I've found that performing it always gets a huge crowd reaction. A footstall looks flashy—and that might be reason enough to learn it! However, it also promotes teamwork, while at the same time teaching your dog balance.

MATERIALS REQUIRED

• Running shoes

BEFORE YOU BEGIN

Working on footstall requires your dog to already know how to sit (page 37) on cue.

INSTRUCTIONS

Take a pair of running shoes and place either your right or left hand inside of them to hold them steady. Sit down, bend your knees, and place the shoes on your knees, with the bottoms facing up. Have your dog in a sit just in front of you. **A**

Lure your dog up onto the shoes. **B** When all four paws are up, mark with a "yes!" and reward. Repeat this step several times over short sessions. At first your dog might take one step at a time to get on the shoes, but eventually you want to progress to him hopping up onto the shoes with all four paws. You'll need to stay at this step until your dog is able to jump, rather than step, onto the shoes.

Next, place your dog in a sit in front of you. Hold the shoes in one hand, place them on your knees, and lie on your back. Lure him up onto the shoes. **C** Mark with a "yes!" and reward when he jumps up. Repeat this step until he is easily jumping up on the shoes. This is great practice to ensure he can balance on your shoes when they are slightly less stable.

The last step is to put your shoes back on your feet. Have your dog sit in front of you and bring your knees toward your chest so that your feet are angled at 45 degrees. This will make it easier for him to jump up. **D**

Say your cue, then lure him to jump up onto your feet. As he lands on your shoes, mark with a "yes!" and bring your feet up. Reward and hold them steady.

Keep practicing until you and your dog are both comfortable!

BACKSTALL

This trick requires trust from both the human and the dog. It can be easier to have a helper, but it can be done independently as well, and practicing this trick can help build a stronger bond between the two of you. You may find it helpful to use a wall or barrier behind you when first starting out.

INSTRUCTIONS

Start with your dog next to you, on either your right or left side. You should be down on your hands and knees, but if you have a tiny dog, you may want to start by lying flat on your stomach first. Press your feet against the wall. If your dog is on your left, use your right hand to lure him up, or vice versa. **A**

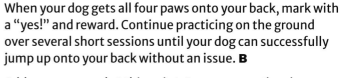

When your dog gets all four paws onto your back, mark with a "yes!" and reward. Continue practicing on the ground over several short sessions until your dog can successfully jump up onto your back without an issue. **B**

Add your cue word at this point. Say your cue, then lure your dog up on your back. Practice a few times, then try just cuing the dog without the lure. When he jumps up on your back, mark with a "yes!" and give him a jackpot.

The next step is to practice on your feet. (If you started on your stomach, move to your hands and knees first before attempting to stand.) It's very important to be sure your back is flat to give your dog a nice solid platform. **C**

Cue your dog to jump on your back, mark, and reward. Continue to practice until your dog can easily hop up on your back. **D**

TROUBLESHOOTING

If your dog is a little unsure about placing all four paws on your back, help build his confidence by breaking down the first step and rewarding him for putting one paw on your back, then two, etc.

If you have any issues while standing, widen your stance to make yourself a bit sturdier for your dog. This also decreases the height your dog has to jump, making it easier for him.

LIMP

Whenever people talk about famous dog actors, the number one dog that always comes to mind is Lassie. Lassie's famous "limp" trick is one that requires a fair amount of muscle memory, so don't get discouraged if it takes a little longer for your dog to pick it up. Teaching this trick and then performing it is sure to brighten anyone's day!

BEFORE YOU BEGIN

Working on limp requires your dog to already know how to shake a paw (page 49) on cue.

INSTRUCTIONS

Have your dog start in front of you in a stand and ask for his paw. **A**

If he sits, just be patient and reposition him. Continue to practice in short sessions until your dog can successfully give you his paw while he is standing on all fours, instead of trying to sit.

The next step is to present your hand flat and perpendicular to the floor. Ask your dog for his paw, and as he goes to swipe your hand and holds his paw in the air, mark with a "yes!" and reward. **B**

You will need to spend a fair amount of time on this step, building duration for holding his paw in the air.

The hardest part of teaching your dog to limp is duration. To build duration, slowly increase the time your dog holds his paw in the air before marking and rewarding. Some dogs may require you to break this step down into second or half-second increments. Be patient, as building muscle memory can take some time. **C**

Once your dog is able to hold his paw in the air for several seconds, take a step back from your dog and present your hand. Your dog should take a step forward and give you his paw. Keep practicing this until he can limp a few steps forward. Once your dog is successfully limping, name the trick and practice using your cue.

SCOOT

So, your dog can crawl forward, but what about backward? This super-cute trick is always a favorite to perform, and a hit for crowds big or small! As an added bonus, teaching this trick can help your dog learn rear-end awareness and increase strength in his back legs, which can be incredibly useful in other dog sports, such as agility or disc.

BEFORE YOU BEGIN

Working on scoot requires your dog to already know how to lie down (page 38) on cue.

INSTRUCTIONS

Start with your dog in a down in front of you. **A**

Using a piece of food, place your hand in between his paws and gently push it into his chest. This should cause him to look down and shuffle backward. Mark with a "yes!" as he moves back and reward. Repeat this step several times over short two- to three-minute sessions.

Once your dog is easily shuffling backward, try to lure him the same way, but with no food. If he moves back, mark with a "yes!" and reward.

Say your cue word, such as "scoot," then immediately lure him without food. When he scoots backward, mark and give him a jackpot! Repeat this step a few times. **B**

The next step is to cue him to scoot, then wait for him to offer the behavior. This will take lots of patience. Once he scoots back, mark and reward! If he's having trouble, help him out by luring without food another time or two, then try without the lure again.

As your dog gets better at the behavior, wait a little longer before rewarding to get some duration.

TROUBLESHOOTING

If your dog is having an issue with the backward motion, consider the surface you're asking him to perform on. If you're on a hard surface, try moving to a carpeted area.

Some dogs will pop up when you attempt to lure. Take your time and, if needed, reward the slightest motion backward to break the behavior down into super small steps.

OPEN AND CLOSE THE DOOR

Teaching a dog to open a door and close it behind himself can be extremely useful! He will be able to let himself in and out of rooms without requiring your assistance, so if you're comfortable on the couch and your dog is in another room, there's no need to get up. A dog that can open a door is also very helpful if your hands are full!

To make opening the door easier for the dog, I suggest using a rope or long sock. It's helpful if your dog is familiar with the game of tug before starting this trick. Practice each step over a few short sessions. I recommend not teaching these in the same session.

MATERIALS REQUIRED

- Rope or sock

BEFORE YOU BEGIN

Working on open and close the door requires your dog to already know how to tug (page 16) and nose touch (page 53) on cue.

INSTRUCTIONS

OPEN THE DOOR

Tie the rope or sock to the existing handle on the door of a cabinet. **A**

With your dog next to you, encourage him to interact with the rope—move it around, and urge him to "get it!" **B**

Make it super exciting, then stop briefly and give him a chance to play with it. The first time he goes to mouth the rope or sock, mark with a "yes!" and reward. For the first few attempts, mark and reward all efforts to grab the rope. Ignore any interactions made with his paws.

Next, raise your criteria by waiting until he tugs on the rope to reward. **C**

When he does, it should cause the door to open, even if only a little bit. When he gets the door open, even a few inches, mark with a "yes!" and give him a jackpot.

Continue practicing until your dog has successfully pulled the door open. At this point, when you can predict he will tug hard enough to fully open the door, you can add a name to the behavior and practice with your cue.

CLOSE THE DOOR

Start with the door open. Encourage your dog to touch the door with his nose. **D**

If he needs help, you can use a sticky note to give him a place to "target" his nose. When his nose touches the door, even lightly, mark with a "yes!' and reward.

At first, reward even the smallest of touches, but as your dog gets more confident, wait for a stronger nose touch. If you have added a sticky note on the door, you can fade it out by making the sticky note gradually smaller before removing it altogether.

Continue practicing until your dog is successfully closing the door with his nose. When he is using enough pressure to fully close the door, you can add a cue to the behavior and practice using the cue. **E**

HOOPED ARMS

This trick is fun, flashy, and fast-moving. Because dogs love to jump, this trick is ideal for burning off some of that extra energy in a positive way. It will engage your dog's brain, provide physical exercise, and simultaneously strengthen your bond, while showing off some serious skills!

BEFORE YOU BEGIN

Working on hooped arms is easier if your dog already knows how to over arms (page 66).

INSTRUCTIONS

The good news for this trick is that if your dog has mastered the over arms trick, you've already taught him the first step! Similar to how you taught over arms, return to the wall; however, instead of placing one arm out against the wall, this time create a circle with your arms, very low to the ground.

Ask your dog to stay and place food on the opposite side of your arms. **A**

Cue him to get the food, mark with a "yes!" when he goes through your arms, and reward again once he's completely through. **B**

Next, set your dog up the same way, but this time do not place any food on the ground. Cue your dog to jump through using your cue for him to get the food, and reward when he does so. **C** Practice this over several short sessions, and gradually raise your hooped arms higher and higher against the wall, a few inches at a time.

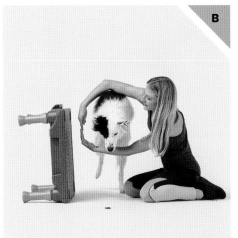

Once your dog is successfully jumping through, start to move away from the wall and keep practicing.

TROUBLESHOOTING

If your dog has trouble jumping through your circled arms, try making the area between your arms larger to start. Once he's easily jumping through the "large" hoop, you can slowly decrease the size.

REBOUND

This is a dynamic and athletic trick that can be done independently or as a team! It's fun, flashy, looks impressive, and is always a crowd-pleaser. Rebound is a fast-paced trick that is enjoyable and rewarding for both partners.

MATERIALS REQUIRED

- Cot or board (about the size of a small couch cushion, or a Klimb platform works well)
- Agility jump, pole, or propped-up broom handle

BEFORE YOU BEGIN

Working on rebound requires your dog to already know how to jump in arms (page 75) on cue.

INSTRUCTIONS

REBOUND

It's important to do some groundwork for this trick before you have your dog start any serious jumping. Start by setting up the cot or board at a 45-degree angle.

You can use a couch or something heavy behind the board to keep it still. Place the agility jump or pole horizontally in front of the flat surface. How far off the ground you place the pole depends on the size of the dog. You want to place the jump or pole just far enough away from the board so that your dog's paws will hit the surface on the other side without touching the ground.

The first step is to lure your dog over the jump. Stand beside him, take a piece of food, and lure your dog's front paws over the pole. Mark with a "yes!" when his paws hit the board on the other side and reward. **A**

Repeat this several times over short sessions until your dog is consistently hitting the board with his front paws. Remove the food lure and try luring with just your hand or finger. Mark and reward when he is successful.

Next, lure your dog over the jump using just your hand gesture. This time, when he hits the board, keep your arm moving in a semicircle motion, turning the dog toward you. He should continue over the jump, and his back paws should hit the surface. Mark with a "yes!" and then reward at the end of the semicircle, after he has jumped back over the bar.

Continue to practice this until he is jumping over the pole and making a smooth semicircle motion off of the surface. Keep practicing until he is pushing off the surface with his rear legs, then add your cue! **B**

Remove the jump or pole and continue to practice without it in front of the board. **C** Once your dog is successful, you can start to practice on other surfaces and continue building up his confidence with the trick.

It's important to practice this trick on both sides, so spend plenty of time working with your dog on both sides to build this skill!

REBOUND AS A TEAM

Performing this trick as a team requires a few extra steps.

To start, cue your dog to jump into your arms. As he does, and his front paws hit your body, throw some food in front of you. This will cause him to turn his body and push off you to get to the food. When he does, mark with a "yes!" and his reward is the food that has been tossed.

You can also accomplish the same result using toys as a reward, if your dog is more toy-driven. **D**

Add your cue and keep practicing! As you practice and your dog is successful in pushing off you, stop throwing food and instead reward after he has completed the rebound. **E**

FAKE PEE

This is a great party trick that will make all your friends and family laugh, especially when you send your dog to a potted plant or a friend's pant leg and cue him to lift his leg. It's a trick that generally catches everyone by surprise, but quickly becomes a party favorite once guests realize that your dog isn't actually going potty indoors!

This is a trick that I've also seen used in several live shows and pretty much every Hollywood dog has mastered it. In a few short steps, your dog will soon be "peeing" with the best of them!

MATERIALS REQUIRED

- Platform

INSTRUCTIONS

Take a piece of food and lure your dog over the platform. Focus on getting only one back foot up on the surface, and when the paw lands on the platform, mark with a "yes!" and reward. **A** Practice this step over a few short sessions. The platform should be a few inches off the ground to start.

Once your dog is consistently offering to target his paw to the surface without the lure, try removing the platform. Lightly tap the leg your dog has been lifting to encourage him to lift it up, and when he does, mark with a "yes!" and reward. Keep practicing over several short sessions. **B**

Continue practicing and delay rewarding to increase duration. Once your dog can hold up his leg for a few seconds, you can name the behavior ("oops" is a great cue!) and start to fade out the tap of your hand to your dog's leg. Do this by cuing your dog and waiting a second or two to see if he will lift his leg. If he doesn't, lightly tap it and reward when he lifts his leg. Then try again. Your dog should begin to realize that he will get his reward faster if he performs the trick before you help him out. **C**

TROUBLESHOOTING

If your dog is having trouble with targeting his back foot, start with a flat target instead of one a few inches off the ground so he gets used to having to place his back paw on a different surface. You can also use a larger platform to give your dog a bigger area to target. It can be challenging for a dog to use his back feet to target —just be patient . . . he'll get there!

GRAB TAIL

Around and around he goes. Some people may not think a dog grabbing his tail can be a trained behavior, but it sure gives people a great laugh! Teaching your dog to grab his tail can provide great body awareness, while simultaneously increasing flexibility.

BEFORE YOU BEGIN

Working on grab tail requires your dog to already know how to lie down (page 38) on cue.

INSTRUCTIONS

The first step is working on getting your dog comfortable with you touching his tail. Start with your dog in a down. As you touch his tail, mark with a "yes!" and reward. Practice this several times until your dog doesn't show any discomfort. It may take several short sessions if your dog is hesitant with handling. **A**

Next, with your dog in a down, pick up his tail and wait for him to lick at your hand or go to grab it from you. **B**

As he does, mark with a "yes!" and reward. You will likely need to practice this several times over a few sessions, so take your time.

Once your dog is able to grab hold of his tail when you're holding it, practice with him in a down and simply tap his tail with your hand, let go, and wait for him to grab it. **C**

When he grabs his tail, be sure to mark with a "yes!" and reward. Start to build duration by increasing the amount of time before marking and rewarding. You may need to break this down very slowly, and increase the time he holds his tail by only a second at a time.

Once he is consistently grabbing his tail in a down, and you have built some duration in holding his tail (a few seconds), start to add a verbal cue. I use "get it," along with a hand motion. **D**

Be sure to also practice this trick while your dog is standing once he is comfortable performing it while in a down. Make sure to mark and reward his efforts—he should be able to easily pick up the trick in the new position but go at his pace. In no time, you'll have a dog that can easily grab his tail and spin in a circle on cue.

LOOK BACK

This is a fantastic trick that works on your dog's coordination and, as with all tricks, will also help strengthen the bond between you. This behavior is commonly used in canine freestyle routines but can be used to entertain anyone!

BEFORE YOU BEGIN

Working on look back requires your dog to already know how to sit (page 37) and stay (page 13) on cue.

INSTRUCTIONS

Have your dog sit in front of you, and ask him to stay. Walk behind him, and reward him for staying in place. Make sure you are standing very close to him. **A**

Slowly shift your body to the left, using your left arm, if necessary, to draw his attention in that direction. **B** As he turns his head to look at you, mark with a "yes!" and reward. For this trick it's important that your dog remains in position for his reward rather than getting up to get it.

Repeat the same process on the right side. **C**

Continue to practice on both sides over several short sessions until your dog can easily turn his head in both directions to look back at you. Add a verbal cue for each side, which will help when you want to add some distance to the behavior.

The final step is to add some distance! Take this slowly, only increasing the space between you and your dog by a step at a time. You can use both the verbal and visual cue to aid your dog.

TROUBLESHOOTING

If your dog is getting confused, practice exclusively on one side at a time. Once he's got that down, you can train the other side. After he is comfortable looking over both shoulders, practice them together.

BOUNCE

This is one of my dogs' favorite tricks. It's very high-energy and really showcases a dog's enthusiasm for performing! Teaching your dog to jump into the air is fun to photograph and is also helpful to know for other tricks, like jump rope or dog sports.

INSTRUCTIONS

Have your dog in a stand in front of you. Hold a piece of food in your hand above your dog's head, just out of reach, and encourage him to get it. As he jumps to get the food, mark with a "yes!" and reward.

In the beginning, reward all of his efforts. If he gets all four feet off the ground, mark with a "yes!" and give him a jackpot. **A**

When your dog can consistently jump in the air and all four paws leave the ground, begin to use both hands to encourage him to jump. **B**

With practice, you can add a verbal cue, such as "jump" or "bounce."

SUPER TRICK DOG

The following tricks are ones that many dogs will find a bit more difficult than those in the preceding chapters.

These are the flashy, showy tricks that impress everyone when your dog performs them. Being able to complete these skills gives such a sense of accomplishment to the human handler and can encourage further bonding between the dog and his human partner.

Most of these behaviors require a prerequisite trick in order to be successful, so it is recommended to start with tricks from the easier sections. Once your dog has the building blocks required, these difficult tricks are much easier for him to learn.

SKATEBOARD

Your dog will be the coolest dog at the park! This is a super-fun trick to use for live performances or just to make your neighbors smile. Teaching your dog how to ride a skateboard is not only flashy, but it also helps teach him body awareness. I have taught numerous dogs how to ride a skateboard, and each one learns it in a different way, at his own pace. However, by using the basics of each technique you will have success with this trick.

MATERIALS REQUIRED

- Skateboard
- Leash

INSTRUCTIONS

GETTING ON THE BOARD

Step one is to get your dog used to the board. This can be done by using your dog's meal. Place the board in front of the dog, and mark with a "yes!" and reward him for touching the board, moving the board, or otherwise interacting with it. **A**

TIP: *With your dog around, explore the board's sounds, such as flipping it over, rolling the wheels with your hands, moving it back and forth. Reward the dog as you do. This will allow the dog to have a positive experience with any sound or movement the board might make.*

Next, focus on getting your dog's paws on the board. Hold the board steady and lure your dog up onto it. Mark with a "yes!" and reward all efforts where he gets a paw on.

When he is comfortable with one paw, hold out for two, and so on, until all four paws are on the board. Take your time—this may take several short sessions. Add a cue, such as "hop on," to get on the board once he can easily hop up.

Once your dog is up on the board with all four paws, attach a leash to the front of the board and pull it carefully toward you. **B**

Keep the motion very slow at first, and the movements forward very small. Mark with a "yes!" and reward him for staying on the board. Practice this until your dog is comfortable standing on the board while it is moving slowly.

Gradually add some speed, making sure to keep your dog's safety in mind.

RIDING THE BOARD

The next step is to start your dog behind the board. Do not hold the board in place when you cue him to jump onto it. **C** The board will move forward naturally when he jumps on, and you want to mark with a "yes!" and give him a jackpot for staying on the board when it moves forward.

Once he is confident enough to stay on the board while it is moving, it's time to teach him how to move the board on his own.

While your dog is standing on the board, use a piece of food and gently apply some pressure at his nose until one paw goes off the board. Mark with a "yes!" and reward a few times, one piece after another. Repeat this a few times. **D**

Once your dog can drop one paw with minimal pressure, start to move the board forward. When your dog takes a step with the paw that is on the ground, mark with a "yes!" and give him a jackpot. Continue to practice, rewarding each step. **E**

As he gets more comfortable, you will notice that your dog will start to push the board himself, so you can slowly ease off pulling the board forward.

Reward in tiny increments and be generous—this is difficult! If he takes one step on his own, reward that a few times, then hold out for an extra step. This part of the trick may take a bit of extra time but will be well worth the effort. At this point, you can name the behavior. I usually use "board."

JUMP ROPE

This trick has always been a favorite for my dogs to perform—and for me to teach! Their enthusiasm is evident, as the dogs practically vibrate in excitement when I bring out the jump rope! This trick is fun, flashy, and always a crowd-pleaser. You can have someone help you turn the rope, tie the rope to a doorknob if you don't have a second person . . . or, eventually, you can jump with your dog!

MATERIALS REQUIRED

- Jump rope

INSTRUCTIONS

First, tie your jump rope to something solid and low to the ground. Have your dog sit in front of you, and tighten the rope.

Lure your dog to jump over the rope. Mark with a "yes!" and reward. Repeat this step over multiple short sessions, until your dog is easily jumping back and forth over the rope. This will help acclimate your dog to the rope being under him. **A**

Once he is comfortable jumping over the rope, you can start to add movement to it. Have your dog off to one side of the rope. Lure him over, and as he jumps, move the rope under him toward the side he jumped from. Mark with a "yes!" and reward. **B**

Practice this step until he can easily jump over as you move the rope to the side. It may require several sessions.

Keep practicing this until you can do a full circle over your dog with the rope, then work on adding multiple circles! Your jump rope will be the cue for this trick.

TROUBLESHOOTING

In some cases, you may need to spend some extra time getting your dog used to the rope. If this is necessary, I recommend having him in a sit by your side while you move the rope up and down and all around, rewarding him as you do so.

You can also teach bounce (page 131) if your pup has extra hops and enjoys jumping!

WALK ON HIND LEGS

This trick is all about building muscle memory and strength in your dog's back legs and hips. It requires more patience than some tricks and lots of extra practice! Teaching your pup to walk on his back legs is both entertaining and good exercise.

INSTRUCTIONS

With your dog in front of you, take a piece of food and lure him up until he is standing on his hind legs. **A** Immediately mark with a "yes!" and reward. No duration is required just yet, so rewarding as soon as your dog is standing is a good idea to help build his confidence in the behavior. **B**

Keep practicing over multiple short sessions until it is clear that holding the position is becoming easier for him. Make sure you avoid having your dog hang on to you for support, as this could make the trick more difficult to teach as you go along.

Once your dog can stand easily, start to ask for a bit of duration. Do this by having several pieces of food in your hand. Use them to rapidly reward, one piece after another, while he is standing on his hind legs.

Once your dog can stand on his hind legs for a few seconds, start to add movement forward. Do this by luring him up and taking a step back. **C** He should move forward to follow the lure. Some dogs find it easier to walk backward on their hind legs, so go slowly and only ask for one step at a time. **D** Once your dog can take a few steps forward, name the trick. Keep practicing, using your verbal cue, and build more duration!

PUT TOYS AWAY

This trick looks impressive when you have company and is also a useful skill for your dog to learn. When your dog leaves his toys everywhere, it can be helpful to teach him to clean them up! To make it easier for your dog, start with a large box so your dog is sure to be successful. Once he's learned to target the box with the toy, changing to a smaller box is easier!

MATERIALS REQUIRED

- Large box (a large plastic storage container would work well)
- Small box (the box you eventually want to use to store the dog's toys)
- Toys (stuffed animals, rope toys, and tennis ball–sized balls work well for most dogs)

BEFORE YOU BEGIN

Working on put toys away requires your dog to already know how to retrieve (page 153) and hold object (page 157) on cue.

INSTRUCTIONS

Have your dog sit on one side of the large box while you sit on the other side. **A**

Hand him a toy, and once he has taken it, present a piece of food to him. When he drops the toy in the large box, mark with a "yes!" and reward. Repeat this over several short sessions until he is dropping the toy in the box nearly every time. **B**

Next, toss the toy a very short distance from the box and have your dog retrieve it. Hold your hands above the large box, and when he brings it back to you, wait until he drops the toy in the box. When he does, mark with a "yes!" and reward. **C**

Slowly increase the amount of distance between the toy and the box by a foot or so. Repeat this step multiple times, and when he is successfully dropping the toy in the box almost every time, add a cue, such as "tidy up."

At this point, you can switch to a smaller box and back up a step if needed, but you should be able to add your cue back soon.

HUG LEG

This trick has a feel-good, heartwarming "aww" factor that appeals to every dog person! Aside from being adorable, it will also help build up your dog's core muscles. This is a pretty simple trick on its own that can be developed into a much more difficult trick, such as hugging an object (page 147), which requires several tricks to be combined into one.

BEFORE YOU BEGIN

Working on hug leg will be easier if your dog already knows how to sit pretty (page 65) on cue.

INSTRUCTIONS

Stand next to your dog and present your leg.

Use a piece of food and lure him up into a sit pretty. Mark with a "yes!" and reward when he rests his paws on your leg. **A**

If your dog does not have a "sit pretty," you will need to spend some time building up his core strength by practicing this step over several short sessions.

Next, wiggle your leg carefully until his paws wrap around your leg. Mark with a "yes!" and reward. Practice this several times over multiple sessions until he automatically wraps his paws around your leg without any extra assistance. At this point, you can add your cue! I use "hug" for this behavior. **B**

HUG OBJECT

Using hug leg as a building block, you can eventually teach your dog to hug something else. This trick is difficult because it requires a lot of balance. Keep in mind that you want him to be as comfortable as possible with this trick, so make sure to spend a fair amount of time building up your dog's core muscles.

MATERIALS REQUIRED

- Stuffed animal (about half the dog's size is suggested)

BEFORE YOU BEGIN

Working on hug object requires your dog to already know how to sit pretty (page 65), hold object (page 157), and hug leg (page 144) on cue.

INSTRUCTIONS

While your dog is sitting in front of you, cue him to sit pretty and then hand him an object, but do not let go of it. **A**

Hold it in front of him and wait a moment. Mark with a "yes!" and reward when he successfully wraps his paws around the object. Practice this over several short sessions.

Next, work on building duration, making sure you are still holding the object. Mark with a "yes!" and reward after your dog holds the stuffed animal for a second or two. Continue to practice until he can hold the object for several seconds. **B**

Now you're ready to put it all together! As your dog is holding the object with his paws, use your "hold" cue to get him to take the top of the object in his mouth. Immediately mark with a "yes!" and reward. Practice this several times.

At this point you can start letting go of the object and start increasing the amount time he holds it before marking and rewarding. Once he can hold the object for a few seconds, you can add your "hug" cue!

TROUBLESHOOTING

It may take several attempts for your dog to get his paws fully around the object, so if that happens, mark and reward smaller attempts. Using a larger stuffed animal can make this step easier, as it will encourage him to move his paws more than a smaller one would.

WALKING HANDSTAND

Did you know a walking handstand is actually easier for a dog to perform than a stationary one? This is definitely one of the most impressive tricks, especially when the human half isn't even able to accomplish it! Teaching a handstand can be very time-consuming. It is another trick that will help develop your dog's balance and core strength.

MATERIALS REQUIRED

- Platform

BEFORE YOU BEGIN

Working on walking handstand is easier if your dog already knows how to back up (page 72) on cue.

INSTRUCTIONS

Starting this trick can sometimes be challenging. Using a low platform (very close to the ground, if necessary) and eventually working your way up to a higher platform will make teaching this trick easier.

Have your dog back up onto the platform. Ideally you want your dog to raise both back paws into the air and land on the elevated surface. You can achieve this by asking your dog to back up, then mark with a "yes!" and reward him when he lifts his back paws onto the platform. **A** If this is too big for a first step, you can tilt the platform forward so that it is angled, which makes backing up onto it much easier.

If your dog doesn't understand how to back up, you can start him on the platform and lure only his front paws off of it, rewarding for position (back feet up/front feet on the floor) or

place a piece of food at his nose and gently push backward to encourage the "back up" movement. **B**

Continue to mark and reward for his back paws on the platform until he is successfully lifting his paws up on his own. **C**

Once your dog is easily placing his back paws up on the platform, place your arm up and have your dog back his paws up onto your arm. Mark with a "yes!" and reward when his paws touch your arm. **D**

If your dog is having trouble, try placing your arm behind his back foot, and use food to lure him backward. When he lifts his back paw, place your arm under it and reward him as soon as his paw touches your arm. Once you are able to get one back foot on your arm, the second one should follow.

TIP: *You can do this step off the platform if needed, but I have always had more success with the dog already on the platform.*

As you practice, you can start to teach your dog to target your arm with his back paws on cue. A few cue options are "handstand," "bottoms up," or "spider."

As he has more and more success, ask your dog to back up onto the elevated platform, then cue your dog to target your arm. Start very close to your dog and gradually build up distance. Remember to reward his successes! The more you practice, the stronger and better your dog will become. Once your dog is popping into the handstand consistently, you can remove the platform. **E**

RETRIEVE

Not only is this a great life skill, but a solid retrieve can also be helpful in many scenarios. For example: fetching dropped items or items low to the ground if it is difficult for the dog's owner to bend down, getting his leash to take a walk, or even just doing something fun, like bringing the television remote.

MATERIALS REQUIRED

- An item your dog likes that is easy for him to pick up, such as a toy rope

BEFORE YOU BEGIN

Working on retrieve requires your dog to already know how to nose touch (page 56) and hold object (page 157) on cue.

INSTRUCTIONS

Place an item your dog is familiar with and really likes on the ground in front of him. Mark with a "yes!" and reward any attempt he makes to put the item in his mouth. **A** Practice this several times over multiple short sessions, rewarding each attempt that is more successful than the previous, until your dog is picking up the object easily. Make sure you aren't expecting too much too fast, and give your dog lots of opportunities to be successful.

Next, place the item on the ground and wait for your dog to pick it up. Once he does, hold out the palm of your hand very close to your dog and cue a nose touch. **B** When your dog presses his nose into your palm, wait a few seconds, then mark with a "yes!" and calmly take the item from his mouth and reward. If he drops the item before you get the chance to take it, on the next attempt, take it from him a little sooner.

Repeat this several times over multiple short sessions until your dog is successfully retrieving the item to your hand.

Now practice by throwing the item a foot or two away and having your dog bring it back by cuing a nose touch. Mark and reward each successful attempt. **C** Gradually increase the distance you throw the item by about a foot each time. You can decrease that distance if your dog is having trouble.

At this point, you can name the behavior instead of cuing the nose touch and start to practice with various items.

DANCE

This trick is accomplished by putting two tricks together. It's fun, flashy, and always a crowd favorite. This one requires some extra patience, as it requires quite a bit of coordination, rear-end awareness, and strength to complete it.

BEFORE YOU BEGIN

Working on dance requires your dog to already know how to walk on hind legs (page 140) and orbit (page 96).

INSTRUCTIONS

Start with your dog off to your side. **A** The side your dog starts on depends on which way he is most comfortable when performing the orbit trick.

Have food in both hands and lure your dog into a stand. **B** Slowly lure your dog backward around you. You may need to break up the circle, and have your dog take only a few steps around you before marking with a "yes!" and rewarding.

Practice over several short sessions to allow your dog to gain strength and confidence.

Keep working at it in stages. Once he reaches the halfway point, you'll need to switch the hand you're luring with to complete the circle. **C**

Keep working over several short sessions until your dog can get all the way around you while in a stand. Continue to work at it until you don't need to use both hands to lure. **D**

As you practice, you'll notice that your dog's strength and stamina will improve, and he can make it all the way

around easily. At this point you can add your cue, such as "boogie," "dance," or "twirl."

TIP: *Make sure that when you practice, you avoid offering to help your dog balance. Doing so will make this trick difficult for him to accomplish independently. Focus on building your dog's core strength by rewarding small steps and hold off on completing the full circle until he's ready.*

HOLD OBJECT

This is one of the most adorable, yet also extremely useful, skills you can teach your dog. Once he knows how to hold on to objects, he can help you carry various items, such as grocery bags! It is also a great trick for photos.

   While working on this trick, keep in mind it takes each dog a varying amount of time to accomplish the behavior. Some dogs are very quick to pick it up, while others struggle a bit and require a little more time. The timing of your reward, along with a little patience, will go a long way in helping your dog understand what you're after.

MATERIALS REQUIRED

- PVC pole or similar

* I like to teach this behavior using a hard object. I do this because it will make it easier as you go along to transfer the behavior to any other object.

INSTRUCTIONS

Have your dog sit in front of you. Present the object, and when he goes to sniff/touch/lick it, mark with a "yes!" and reward. **A** If he grabs the object, mark with a "yes!" and give him a jackpot.

At this stage, you are not saying anything while you wait for your dog to perform the correct behavior. You are just looking for him to interact with the object—with his mouth, not his paws. There is no need for duration just yet. **B**

Practice over several short sessions until your dog is grabbing the object and pulling back very slightly. At this point, you want to let go and allow for a second or two of duration. Make sure you mark with a "yes!" before your dog drops the item, and then reward.

Once you have reached a few seconds of duration, add a cue, such as "hold" or "take it." **C**

You can then start practicing with other objects. **D** When you introduce a new object, you may have to back up a step, but you should be able to add your cue back soon. After your dog can hold a few items, you should be able to ask for the behavior right from the beginning.

TROUBLESHOOTING

If your dog is truly having trouble holding a hard object, switching to a softer object in the beginning may help.

CANINE FREESTYLE

Canine freestyle is something I fell in love with after watching Cruft's freestyle competitions. The creativity each team puts into a routine is what drew me in, but it was the relationship between dog and handler that inspired me to get more involved and keep learning. At the time, there really weren't many resources to help me teach the tricks or put together a routine. I learned by trial and error, trusting the process and working on new ways to get to the final behavior.

There are two different versions of canine freestyle: heelwork to music and musical canine freestyle. For the purpose of this book, the focus is on a less formal version of musical canine freestyle—something achievable and fun to do at home!

HEELWORK TO MUSIC (HTM)

Heelwork to Music involves a lot of obedience and very precise heelwork, both stationary and in motion. There are eight different heel positions that are choreographed to music, with the dog and handler turning, moving forward, and moving backward. In HTM, the majority of the routine must be in one of the various heel positions, while about a third of the routine can be freestyle. Heelwork, when it is well done, can be a dance all on its own and is really amazing to watch or perform!

MUSICAL CANINE FREESTYLE

In this version of canine freestyle, only a small portion of the routine needs to involve heelwork on the competition level. The remainder of the routine is a variety of fun and flashy tricks the handler and dog use to create a story for the audience.

Though many teams have set routines they practice to perfection, I personally love to randomly select various sequences that I have trained and then put them to music in many different ways. My dogs get very comfortable switching up tricks and continually practice a wide range of behaviors in order to perform a fun variation of freestyle. So that will be the aim in this chapter: learn the basics of a "routine" and put it to music!

THE MUSIC

In my opinion, one of the most important parts of any freestyle routine is the music! You could have the most spectacular routine, but what if you don't have the perfect song to go along with it? To prevent this from happening, something I have learned over the years is that it's best to build your routine around a song. It's important to pick an appropriate song, not only for the lyrics but also for the location where the performance will be.

Selecting music for your routine is a vital part of creating the mood and atmosphere you'd like to portray to your audience. When figuring out what kind of music to use, you want to envision how you'd like the routine to flow—and pick out important moments you want to highlight using sequences. I often choose songs that use a variety of different tempos and powerful lyrics that can be matched with dynamic tricks.

THINGS TO CONSIDER

TEMPO AND TEMPO CHANGES

Try to find a song that matches both the speed of your performance and your dog's enthusiasm. You can select a song that has a few slower sections, and then some more upbeat moments.

LYRICS

Use the words in your song to help build the routine and give it some context. You can create a story within the routine, or just use specific segments that work within your selected song.

INSTRUMENTALS

If possible, play around with music that gives you instrumental breaks, or even go with a song that is completely instrumental, if it works with your theme.

VARIETY

When choosing music, try to select a song that has many different beats, and avoid those that repeat their lyrics often. You want to aim for something fresh and interesting so your audience continues to engage with your performance.

A FEW CLASSIC FREESTYLE SONGS

What makes a good freestyle song? Well, some of it is in the eye (or ear) of the beholder! But there are some common themes. Let's take a look at a few that work well.

"Footloose" – Kenny Loggins

This is probably the most-used song for canine freestyle. It has everything that makes a great routine! The changes in tempo allow for a variety of transitions and help with keeping a nice flow of slow- and fast-paced tricks.

"Happy" – Pharrell Williams

As the song title says, this song is very happy and allows for an upbeat but calm feel. It's important to get the audience involved in any routine, and giving them lyrics that say "clap along" invites them to get involved.

"Dance Monkey" – Tones and I

This is a slower song that allows for some exciting moments, but overall focuses on slower rhythms. If you have a dog that is calmer while performing tricks, I recommend trying to use songs that fit that energy.

THEMES AND COSTUMES

Choosing a theme for your canine freestyle routine is an amazingly fun part of the process. It will help you decide on all the other elements needed to complete the routine. Personally, I like to start with current events or holidays that fall around the time I want to perform the routine. Most teams that perform also tend to dress up to match the chosen theme. This isn't completely necessary, but it really does add to the performance (even if you're just performing for your friends or neighbors!).

THINGS TO KEEP IN MIND

DOG SAFETY
Dressing up your dog can be adorable and fun, but style should never compromise safety. I personally put only dog-appropriate gear on my pups, such as harnesses, bandanas, boots, and the occasional bow tie. Like Simon Cowell said, "The reason America loves Hero is because he looks like a dog."

HUMAN COMFORT
You'll want to wear something that allows you to move freely. Avoid anything that is too restrictive or revealing to prevent any accidental outfit malfunctions.

FABRIC
For both costumes, you want to make sure you have a breathable, comfortable fabric that stretches and won't easily rip.

INAPPROPRIATE COSTUME CHOICE

Costumes that obstruct your view and impede movement will only interfere with your ability to perform. If the costume has a hood, this can also interfere with your vision, making it hard to keep your dog in your line of sight.

It's equally important for your dog to be able to move freely and see what is going on, so stick to minimalistic options that add to the look you've created for the routine, without causing any visual or movement issues.

APPROPRIATE COSTUME CHOICE

A costume that is properly fitted to your body, with minimal pieces of fabric hanging off it, will allow you to clearly see your surroundings and allow for maximum movement and flexibility. Your dog's costume should complement yours and allow him to move naturally and without any restrictions. His visibility should be clear. Using something like a bandana is simple and clean for a fluid performance. Another option is a dog sport harness that also allows for natural movement.

Take a look at the pirate-themed costumes on page 160 to see how creative you can be while still following these guidelines.

TROUBLESHOOTING

A dragon costume sounds like a fun idea, but such a bulky outfit can and likely will cause numerous issues, including limiting your dog's ability to read your body language.

PUTTING IT ALL TOGETHER

Often the key component to freestyle is the flow of your performance, and this can be fairly tricky to accomplish. There are more than a few ways the routine can be put together, but the following suggestions are how I personally prefer to approach a routine for my various TV shows and performances:

- Get your routine on paper first. Once you have everything written down, break it into sections and practice on your own, without adding the dog into the picture until you have memorized all the behaviors he will be performing and the movements you'll need to make, and you can make it flow nicely on your own. When you feel ready, practice with your dog until you are both comfortable and confident!

- Focus on your dog's strengths. When creating a routine, I like to focus on the dog's strengths, while simultaneously minimizing any weaknesses he may have. This means if a trick the dog doesn't excel at or may need some encouragement to perform would be perfect in a routine, it will be put immediately before a trick he really enjoys. This makes the second trick a reward for performing the first one and really helps keep the rhythm going!

- Provide a final reward. Something I am asked frequently is if I have treats on me, or if I treat my dog during the routine. In many cases I am not able to do this, plus attempting to feed the dog in the middle of the performance could disrupt the flow. However, I do have one treat in my hand that the dog gets once the entire routine has been completed.

- Offer reinforcement in many forms. You can use a prop the dog really enjoys playing with and have him interact with it. For instance, if your dog likes to tug, and tugging fits in your routine, you may be able to add that in as well.

- Enjoy the experience. The ultimate goal while doing freestyle is for both the dog and the handler to have fun and enjoy the experience. Make sure to incorporate tricks that your dog really loves performing so the behaviors themselves are rewarding. When the dog and handler are both engaged and happy, it really shines through in the performance and makes it an even better experience for both the team and audience.

TRANSITION TRICKS

Transition tricks are used to keep the routine flowing and prevent awkward pauses. They are behaviors that are used to link your sequences and help elevate your performance. Transition tricks may include but are not limited to: spin, scoot, back up, and orbit. While watching freestyle routines, I like to count how many transitions the performance includes.

SAMPLE ROUTINES

Grab a piece of paper and play your selected song. As the song plays, pause when there's a break in the music or the lyrics have a dramatic change. At first, focus on a short 30 second routine. This will help season your dog and get him used to performing a sequence of tricks without being rewarded after each trick. Use those moments to time your tricks and moves. Here's an example of a 30-second routine and a full routine:

THIRTY-SECOND ROUTINE

- 0:00 – 0:10 - start - back up - spin - leg weaves

- 0:10 – 0:15 - orbit - footsies

- 0:15 – 0:25 - spin - rebound

- 0:25 – 0:30 - dog catch + spin with dog in arms

FULL ROUTINE

- 0:00 – 0:10 - start - back up - walking handstand - start

- 0:10 – 0:27 - footsies - orbit - backward leg weaves - back up - orbit - leg weaves - spin

- 0:27 – 0:44 - hooped arms - scoot - rebound - scoot - stand forward - orbit

- 0:44 – 1:04 - orbit - leg hug - scoot - over arms

- 1:04 – 1:20 - turn on feet - spin - arm weaves - roll over - jump over body

- 1:20 – 1:51 - setup looks - look left and right - stand orbit - stand forward - rebound

- 1:52 – 2:10 - hooped arms - limp - leg weaves

- 2:10 – end - spin - balance - leg weaves - backward leg weaves - back up - dog catch

ABOUT THE AUTHOR

Sara Carson grew up in Ontario, Canada, where she successfully ran a dog-training facility for more than five years. During that time period, she worked hands-on with hundreds of dogs and owners, teaching dog tricks, obedience, and various dog sport classes.

Since then, Sara has enjoyed training a wide variety of animals, including rats, cats, chickens, goats, and even a wild chipmunk, though she has always been best known for training dogs. She is now recognized as one of the top international trick dog trainers and has received several awards showcasing her achievements.

Sara and her Super Collies have appeared on several TV programs, including *Late Show with David Letterman, The Marilyn Denis Show*, Nickelodeon, and The CW. Sara has aptly earned her title as Celebrity Dog Trainer after placing fifth on Season 12 of *America's Got Talent* in 2017 and again appearing on *America's Got Talent: The Champions* in 2019. Around the country, Sara and her Super Collies can be seen at live events from theaters to sport arenas, including halftime shows at various NBA and NFL games.

In 2017, Sara partnered with Chin and Cheeks LLC to create Puppr, the number one dog-training app on IOS and Android. She continues to live an adventurous life on the road, spending her days performing and teaching dog trick workshops worldwide. Sara and her Super Collies (Hero, Marvel, Groot, Hawkeye, and Fury) can be found online at thesupercollies.com.

THE SUPER COLLIES

HERO   GROOT   FURY

MARVEL   HAWKEYE

ACKNOWLEDGMENTS

None of this would have been possible if it wasn't for my very first dog, Maple. This little cocker spaniel had the most forgiving nature that allowed me to take my time so that the two of us could learn and grow together.

Thank you, Hero, for being the best dog in the world—for being patient and pretty much perfect from day one. You taught me how to be a better trainer in every way. You allowed me to travel and start my career, and have given me more opportunities than I ever could have imagined, including this book!

Thanks to Lindsay Oakley for helping me literally every step of the way. I couldn't have done it without you!

A huge thank-you to Kelly Pratt and Ian Kreidich for the absolutely amazing photos throughout the book.

To Nicole Carpenter for being the best grandma I could have ever asked for—thank you for never thinking my passion was just a hobby, and for always supporting my dog-training obsession from day one.

To my dad, Kevin Carson—thank you for always being there for me, even when I thought you weren't. Your love and support are truly appreciated. I love you so much.

Also, to Quarto and Thom O'Hearn for providing me with this wonderful opportunity to show the world how much fun trick training can be using my methods.

And finally, I can't thank my fans enough for the incredible amount of support and encouragement all of you have provided me. I truly am here today because of you!

DEDICATION

This book is dedicated to my little Loki Man. Thank you for shaping the trainer I am today and giving me the most incredible memories. Every dog I train reflects a part of you.

INDEX